IAN M.C. HOLLINGSBEE

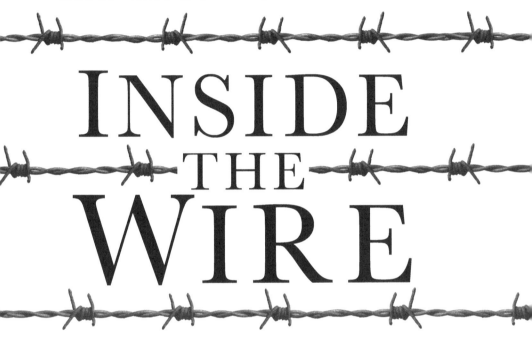

INSIDE THE WIRE

**THE PRISONER-OF-WAR CAMPS AND HOSTELS
OF GLOUCESTERSHIRE 1939–1948**

T0386660

The
History
Press

For my wife, Veronica

We have not eternal allies, and we have no perpetual enemies.
Our interests are eternal and perpetual, and those interests it is our
duty to follow.

Lord Henry Palmerston, 1848

Back cover: painting by 'The Corporal', the late Ken Aitken GAA, of American Military Police with German POW at Moreton-in-Marsh railway station, Gloucestershire. (Reproduced by kind permission of Gerry Tyack of the Wellington Bomber Museum, Moreton-in-Marsh.)

First published 2014
Reprinted 2021

The History Press
97 St George's Place,
Cheltenham, Gloucestershire
GL50 3QB
www.thehistorypress.co.uk

British Library Cataloguing in Publication Data.
A catalogue record for this book is available from the British Library.

ISBN 978 0 7509 5846 2

Typesetting and origination by The History Press
Printed in Great Britain by TJ Books Limited, Padstow, Cornwall

Contents

Acknowledgements

The following people and societies have been helpful with this research and I am most grateful for their support and encouragement: American Red Cross Archives, Maryland, USA; Ann Hettich, Campden & District Historical & Archaeological Society (CADHAS); Barbara Edward, Curator at Sudeley Castle; Barry Simon and Hazel Luxon, Swindon Village Local History Project; Brenda Mitchell and Enid Becker of Gloucester U3A; Eric Miller, Leckhampton Local History Society; Gerry Tyack, Wellington Bomber Museum; Gloucester Coroner's Office; Gloucestershire Archives, Alvin Street, Gloucester; International Committee of the Red Cross in particular Daniel Palmieri, Historical Research Officer, Geneva; Jean Clarke, National Secretary of Catholic Women's League; John Dixon, President of Tewkesbury Historical Society; John Malin, Blockley Antiquarian Society; John Starling, Lt Col, Royal Pioneer Corps Association; Malcolm Barrass, Flt Lt ex-RAFVR(T), RAF History Society; National Monuments Records, Swindon; and The National Archives, Kew. For help with translations, I am indebted to: Gary Costello and Theo Hunkirchen for German translations; Sara Tozzato for Italian translations; and Catherine McLean for French translations. I am grateful to those former prisoners of war and their relations, who were kind enough to share their stories: Joachim Schulze, German POW, and his son Thomas; Theo Hunkirchen and Peter Engler, sons of German POWs; Marilyn Champion, daughter of Italian POW. Thanks also to: Alan Lodge, Alex Smith, Andrew Power, Bill Hitch, Brenda Mitchell, Carol Minter, Clare Broomfield, Colin Martin, David Evans, Ian Hewer, Jack Johnson, Jane Giddings, Jean Clark, Jeremy Bourne, Jerry Mason, Mario Redazione, Peter May, Rosemary Cooke, Shirley Morgan, Stephen Pidgeon, Trefor Hughes, Zosia Biegus — and the many others who have emailed or called with useful clues and information.

A special thank you to two very good friends who have read, encouraged and criticised when needed: Brian Millard and Joachim Schulze. Finally, I owe a great deal of thanks to Roxy Base for her skill and expertise in editing and proofreading my work.

(Sadly both Joachim Schulze and John Malin died towards the end of my research and I am most indebted to them both.)

List of Abbreviations

2 I/C	Second in Command
ATS	Auxiliary Territorial Service (later became the Women's Royal Army Corps)
BAOR	British Army of the Rhine
CO	Commanding Officer
COGA	Control Office for Germany and Austria and Foreign Office, German Section
DCRE	Divisional Chief Royal Engineer
DUKW	US Army amphibious vehicle, known as the Duck
GE	Garrison Engineer
GI	Soldier in US Army
HGV	Heavy Goods Vehicle
ICRC	International Committee of the Red Cross in Geneva
MP	Member of Parliament
NAAFI	Navy, Army & Air Force Institutes (stores & canteens)
NCO	Non-Commissioned Officer
OC	Officer Commanding (Major)
OR	Other Ranks
POW	Prisoner of War
PP	Protected Personnel: involved in camp administration and allowed extra privileges in compensation for delayed transfer/repatriation
RCD	Reserve Clothes Depot
RSD	Reserve Stores Depot
Toc H	Charity supporting military (rest centres etc.)
WAAF	Women's Auxiliary Air Force
WEA	Workers' Educational Association
YMCA	Young Men's Christian Association

German Ranks:

F/w.	Feldwebel = Sergeant
Gefr	Gefreiter = Lance Corporal
H/Fw.	Hauptfeldwebel = Sergeant Major
Lagersprecher	The Camp Speaker, or Spokesperson
Maat	A naval rank closest to Petty Officer
O/Fn.	Oberfähnrich = Senior Officer Cadet
O/Fw.	Oberfeldwebel = Master Sergeant
O/Gefr	Obergefreiter = Senior Lance Corporal
O/Sold.	Private
ROA	Reserveoffizieranwärter = Reserve Officer Candidate
San.Gefr	Sanitätsgefreiter = Lance Corporal (Medical)
S/Arzt.	Stabsarzt = Staff Medical Officer
S/Fw.	Stabsfeldwebel = Warrant Officer or Sergeant Major
S/Wm.	Stabswachtmeister = Master Sergeant (Austrian rank)
Uffz	Unteroffizier = Corporal

The POW Camps in Gloucestershie and their Associated Hostels

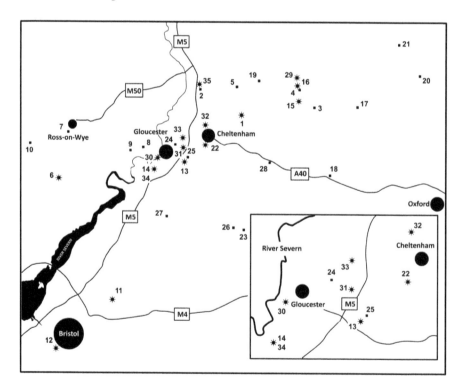

Location of POW camps and associated hostels.

Map Ref.	Camp No.	Main Camps and Administered Hostels	Location	Grid Ref.	Comments
1	37	Sudeley Castle	Winchcombe	SP 030 278	Estate & gardens restored
2		Newtown, Ashchurch	Tewkesbury	SO 904 330	Canterbury Leys PH Beer garden
3		Sezincote		SP 173 311	Exact location not found ★1
4		Moreton-in-Marsh		SP 204 321	Residential housing
5		Alderton		SP 000 332	Exact location not found ★1
6	61	Wynols Hill	Coleford	SO 586 106	Housing estate ★2
7		Ross-on-Wye Drill Hall		SO 601 241	Now Registry Offices
8		Highnam Court		SO 796 192	Private grounds, now only lawns
9		Churcham Court		SO 769 182	Private land, some huts remain
10		Llanclowdy	Herefordshire	SO 492 207	Farmland
11	124	Wapley, Yate	Bristol, S.Glos.	ST 71 79	Location not found, extensive search ★3
12	124a	Ashton Gate	Bristol, S.Glos.	ST 569 717	Camp and caravan site ★3
13	142	Brockworth	Gloucester	SO 890 168	Allotments and housing
14	142	Quedgeley Court	Gloucester	SO 813 153	Industrial area, house no longer exists
15	157	Bourton-on-the-Hill		SP 160 321	Forest area
16	185	Springhill	Blockley	SP 132 357	Private land, some huts remain
17		Over Norton		SP 313 285	Exact location not found ★1
18		Burford		SP 251 121	Misspelt as Burforf on report
19		Stanton		SP 069 342	Exact location not found ★1
20		Bodicote		SP 460 378	Near Banbury, Oxfordshire
21		Horley		SP 418 438	Near Banbury
22	263	Leckhampton Court	Cheltenham	SO 945 193	Now Sue Ryder Home
23		Siddington		SU 050 992	On airfield
24		Elmbridge Court Farm		SO 863 196	Under Glos. Ring Road
25		Hunt Court		SO 903 176	Private house

26		Chesterton		SP 012 003	Farm near Cirencester
27		Woodchester Lodge		SP 839 023	Private house
28		Northleach		SP 111 146	Exact location not found *1
29	327/232	Northwick Park	Blockley	SP 168 365	Business park, some huts remain
30	Coy/554	Newark Farm, Hempstead	Gloucester	SO 816 174	Private accommodation
31	Coy/555	Woodfield Farm	Churchdown	SO 889 190	Pasture
32	Coy/649	Swindon Village	Cheltenham	SO 936 249	Private house
33	702/7	RAF Staverton	Gloucester	SO 884 221	Staverton Airport *4
34	702/148	RAF Quedgeley	Gloucester	SO 810 141?	Kingsway Estate. Exact location not found *1
35	1009	Northway, Ashchurch	Tewkesbury	SO 924 340	Housing estate

Notes:

*1 The exact location of these camps could not be verified or was outside the county.

*2 Wynols Hill near Coleford was also spelt as Wynolls Hill in some reports.

*3 Wapley in Yate Camp 124 & Ashton Gate Camp 124a. The author's intent was to include the two main camps of South Gloucestershire but despite the grid location for Wapley being recorded as ST 71 79 no trace of this camp could be found. Extensive enquiries found no records at the International Red Cross or at The National Archives. Given these facts the author has restricted the research to the current county of Gloucestershire.

*4 Most RAF camps in Gloucestershire housed some German POWs; RAF Innsworth (very close to RAF Staverton) held 127 German POWs in July 1947.

Whilst every effort has been made to ensure precision of grid references used throughout they are for reference only and cannot be used as directions to the exact locations of the camps. Point of interest may be on private or protected land, so please seek landowners permission before gaining access. Readers are encouraged to exercise caution and stay on public footpaths.

Foreword

(Joachim Schulze had agreed to write this Foreword but sadly passed away before it was completed. He did discuss it with his son Thomas, who has sent these words on his father's behalf.)

I am writing a few words on behalf of my father Joachim Schulze who passed away in January 2013 at the age of 86. He spent approximately two years as a POW in England. He was very happy and proud to be mentioned in Ian Hollingsbee's book. The last couple of years of his life he devoted to working on this period of his youth, also writing an article for the *Tewkesbury Historical Society Bulletin 2012*.

The time he spent as a POW in England were very formative years, which helped him revise his war experiences as a young person and especially to deal emotionally with the atrocities he witnessed in the Netherlands in 1944. It convinced him of the importance of being aware of political issues and made him a stern proponent of social democratic values.

He was still able to read most of the chapters of Ian's book and it made him content that this part of history will not be forgotten.

Thomas Schulze, 2014

Preface

Two years ago I spent a night in the old German guard quarters at Colditz Castle in East Germany. Colditz was supposedly an escape-proof German prison fortress for Allied military officers, from all services, who were persistently trying to escape from other prisoner-of-war camps in the occupied territories during the Second World War.

On my return to England I was surprised to note how very little had been written about the many thousands of Italian, German and other Axis forces that were captured and held as prisoners of war (POWs) in Britain, the USA and Commonwealth countries. However, one book by Sophie Jackson entitled *Churchill's Unexpected Guests – Prisoners of War in Britain in World War II* (published in 2010) immediately aroused my curiosity as to whether or not there had been any prisoner-of-war camps within Gloucestershire.

What was it like to be a POW in Britain, knowing that your own country had been defeated? Further, what were the conditions facing these prisoners and how did they cope with captivity?

The source material for this investigation is drawn from a wide range of public records, the personal accounts of those who remember our 'unexpected guests', and from some of those who were themselves the 'unexpected guests'. The final German POWs left these shores in 1948, some sixty-five years ago, so that even the very youngest POW would now be well over 80 years old.

So many times during my enquiries I have been told that a certain named person would have helped me with my research if only they were alive today. Nevertheless, I have tried to maintain the essence of individual witnesses and I am very grateful to the many people who have contacted me, including one Italian and three German POWs who spent some of their war in the county of Gloucestershire.

Searches were conducted at The National Archives at Kew, the National Monuments Records at Swindon, and the International Committee of the Red Cross in Geneva. However, many camp files have not been retained. This has resulted in a significant amount of material for some camps in the county, but very little in relation to others. Records relating to the POWs held by the Americans are not available in the UK and have, therefore, proved difficult to trace. I am most grateful to those American archivists that were approached for their helpful assistance.

I have drawn on the published reports by English Heritage and others which state that each POW camp in Britain was given an official number from 1–1,026. They were then further identified by the International Committee of the Red Cross (ICRC) as being used as base camps, reception camps, special camps (or cages) and Italian, German or other Axis working camps.

Camp numbers were sometimes changed or, as in the case of two of the Gloucestershire camps, were given identical numbers. In addition to these base camps and other types of camp there were significant numbers of hostels throughout the county, one of which housed over 300 POWs. The hostels and billets identified within this work were generally managed by a main camp, sometimes not the closest one. There will be some hostels that have eluded me or I have been unable to locate. Those that remember POWs were children at the time of the Second World War or have been told about the POW hostels by others. Often these hostels were then mistakenly referred to as POW camps.

All the British POW camps within Gloucestershire were working camps and held non-commissioned officers or other ranks. The only exception to this was medical officers who were designated as protected personnel under the Geneva Convention. POWs within these working camps were sent to where their labour was required and where such work was permitted by the second version of the Geneva Convention of 1929. This included agricultural work, which was often seasonal, and other labouring jobs. As a result, POWs were frequently transferred between different locations, hostels, billets or camps.

Ian Hollingsbee, 2014

1

Introduction

Neville Chamberlain, Britain's prime minister, broadcast from the BBC that we were at war with Germany on 3 September 1939. He then appointed Winston Churchill to be the First Lord of the Admiralty.

THE FIRST PRISONERS OF WAR ARRIVE

The first recorded prisoners of war (POWs) in Britain were Luftwaffe aircrew who survived after being shot down or having to crash land, or those submariners who were lucky enough to have survived a Royal Navy or Royal Air Force attack on their German U-boat. Very few U-boat crews that were either torpedoed or depth charged, and subsequently sunk, survived the ordeal. One internet search concluded that out of 40,000 U-boat personnel involved in the Second World War only a quarter lived to see the end of hostilities.

The first U-boat crew to be taken prisoner were in U-boat 27, which was captured in the North Sea with its entire crew on 20 September 1939. This submarine was a type VIIA and had been commissioned on 12 August 1936. The boat had a very short career, however; under her commander, Johannes Franz, she had only one war patrol before being hunted down and sunk, to the west of Lewis in Scotland, by depth charges from the British destroyers *Forester*, *Fortune* and *Faulknor*. Thirty-eight submariners survived that attack and spent the entire war as prisoners of war.[1]

Two POW camps were made available to the War Office in 1939. Camp 1 was situated at Grizedale Hall, Grizedale, Ambleside, in Cumbria. This was a base camp for the reception of captured German or other Axis officers and was described as a 'county house'; it contained thirty huts, with a double perimeter barbed-wire fence and a number of watchtowers. Grizedale Hall was a converted stately home and was, according to reports, both luxurious accommodation and very expensive to run. Colonel Josiah Wedgwood (1872–1943), in a statement to the House of Commons, commented: '… would it not be cheaper to hold them [German POWs] at the Ritz Hotel in London?'

Camp 2 was situated at Glen Mill, Wellyhole Street, Oldham in Lancashire. This was a base camp for other ranks (ORs) and was described as being 'a large cotton mill with its associated weaving huts'. It was later expanded with the addition of a number of Nissen huts.

Sir Winston Leonard Spencer-Churchill became prime minister of the UK following the resignation of Neville Chamberlain on 10 May 1940. At this time Britain stood alone in its active opposition to Adolf Hitler and the German Nazi Party. History records that it was Winston Churchill's resolve in these dark days that inspired the British people in resisting the German threat and standing firm against the enemy onslaught that was to follow.

The early days of the war saw very little need for any extended plans to build POW camps in Britain. Winston Churchill was most reluctant to house POWs in Britain in these early days of the war and, as a result, most were immediately dispatched to Canada and other Commonwealth countries. Britain might well be invaded by the German Army and it was felt unwise to hold a potential standing army of enemy troops within POW compounds.

The movement of German POWs and their Axis partners by ship provoked some very violent demonstrations; they were afraid, and rightly so, that they might be sunk by their own U-boats whilst in convoy across the Atlantic Ocean. Questions were asked in the House of Commons over the legality of taking such a risk under the terms of the Geneva Convention but eventually consent was given to their removal on the grounds of national security.

The Geneva Convention, whilst having no legal safeguards, did provide a framework of rules and expectations on how a prisoner of war was to be treated. The Convention generally worked well because much of a nation's compliance relied on other nations' reciprocity; it was signed by Britain, America, Italy and Germany but not by Russia. The Swiss government, as a neutral nation, provided the inspectors that would keep records of the treatment and facilities faced by the prisoners; this group was known as the International Committee of the Red Cross (ICRC).

The author has relied a great deal on these reports to give a picture of the POW camps within the county of Gloucestershire. One of the key features of the Geneva Convention, made evident in the camp reports presented here, is the neutral status of the military medical personnel, allowing them to be known as protected personnel. These protected personnel were generally of the rank of officer, in charge of the day-to-day running of the POW camp and given much greater freedom of movement than other POWs. The second point the reader should be aware of is that 'other ranking' prisoners could carry out paid work but it could not be directly connected to any war-related operations. Each camp held a copy of the Convention printed in the appropriate language.[2]

The German Government did appeal to the British authorities to reveal the location of POW camps, so that they did not accidentally bomb them, but their request was refused and they were never given this information. It transpired after the war that the German Government had significant knowledge from several aerial reconnaissance photographs they possessed, many of which included the location of POW camps.[3]

 ITALY JOINS THE AXIS

Benito Mussolini, against the advice of his ministers, took Italy into the war on 10 June 1940 and thus became part of the Axis with Germany and her partners. History records that the reason Mussolini and his Fascists decided to go to war was to gain territory through Algiers and Greece, and then to confront the British colonies in her bases in North and East Africa where the Italian and British Imperial territories often shared a common border.[4]

The Italian Army, striking from Abyssinia, mounted raids into Sudan, Kenya and Somaliland with some 91,000 Italian troops and an additional 182,000 from their African territories. They made great advances, including inroads into British Egypt, before their fortunes took a turn for the worse.

In December 1940, what was for the Allies to be a small exploratory raid by 7th Australian Division supported by British forces, codenamed Operation Compass, turned into a full-scale rout. In just a few days, over 38,000 Italians were captured. As if this were not enough, the 13th British Corps then encircled the retreating Italian 10th Army, taking a further 25,000 prisoners. As the British Foreign Secretary, Anthony Eden, was reported as saying: 'Never has so much been surrendered by so many to so few.' This first influx of Italian POWs created a big logistical problem for the British Government.[5]

In 1941, Germany formed its 'Africa Corps' under Field Marshal Erwin Johannes Eugen Rommel (1891–1944). He was well respected by his men and treated all Allied prisoners under the terms of the Geneva Convention. The Italian Army was very poorly led and the German Africa Corps was sent to bolster up the Italian campaign and to get them out of the mess they found themselves in. By August 1941, however, there were well over 200,000 Italian prisoners.

America declared war on Japan on 8 December 1941 and Hitler then declared war on the US on 11 December, due to Germany's treaty with Japan. American forces joined the British in invading French North Africa in an operation codenamed Operation Torch on 8 November 1942, which again resulted in a significant number of Axis POWs.

With America joining the push into southern Italy it was not long before Marshal Badoglio, who had seen the overthrow of Benito Mussolini's Fascist government, surrendered on 8 September 1943. One report states: 'They were all too willing to surrender to the British troops.'

With so many captured it became essential to build suitable camps to house them. At the start of the North African campaign, Operation Torch, most captives were sent to camps in South Africa and other African British dependencies such as Uganda, Rhodesia (now Zimbabwe), Kenya and Tanganyika. In addition some were sent as far away as Australia, Canada and India. Initially this was for logistical reasons in an effort to reduce the cost of feeding such high numbers. It should be remembered that there were 130,000 Germans taken prisoner after the surrender of Tunisia on 13 May 1943.[6]

Holding German POWs in Britain was still a state of affairs that many feared, especially as German invasion remained a great threat and real possibility, but there was also a growing need for labour as more and more people enlisted into the armed services. German POWs were quickly transported to Canada and later, after America joined the war, to the USA.

The armed services had helped in Britain with the annual harvest but they were now required for war duties. With some reluctance it was decided, after much persuasion from the Ministry of Agriculture & Fisheries, that the Italians should be used to fulfil this labour shortage. The officers, however, who did not have to work under the terms of the Geneva Convention (1929), were sent to camps in India and other Commonwealth countries.

It is perhaps necessary to look at the stereotypical view of the Italian POWs as poor peasant types who avoided work, based not on facts but on the prejudices of the 1940s. Italians generally were seen as a docile labour force who could be used to fill labour vacancies in accordance with the Geneva Convention, and it was with this attitude that the records now show that there was a great reluctance to repatriate captives after their countries had surrendered.

The truth of the matter was that the Italians were just as effective in combat as any other soldier but it is also true that they were poorly led, poorly equipped, and many were conscripted and reluctant to join their Fascist leaders. It was only after the defeat of Germany had allowed German POWs and others to replace them as a labour force that the Italians were eventually repatriated. (*See* Chapter 5)

Taking that Italy surrendered in 1943, there were to be 157,000 Italian captives sent to Britain during this stage of the war. With such vast numbers it is interesting to note that there were to be 666 POW camps in the USA and twenty-one in Canada before the war was over. The largest Italian camp was at Zonderwater in South Africa, which was so vast that it has been described as the size of a city; it was the largest Italian POW camp, holding nearly 100,000 prisoners of war before it eventually closed down on 1 January 1947.[7]

This early victory in North Africa produced 50,000 prisoners to be housed in Britain, 3,000 to be sent by 8 July 1941 in order to help build the POW camps to house these new prisoners. One of the reasons Churchill had decided to accept them was the extreme shortage of labour. Two camps were prepared as transit camps: one at Prees Heath, Shropshire (Camp 16), and another at Lodge Moor in Yorkshire (Camp 17).

The accounts about these prisoners refer to their very poor state of health and that they were commonly lousy. The Minister of Health was concerned for public safety regarding prevalent infectious diseases including malaria, typhoid and dysentery, not to mention the infestation of body and hair lice.

Seven more labour camps were then built, the nearest to Gloucestershire being Camp 27 at Ledbury in Herefordshire.

THE GERMANS ARRIVE 'EN MASSE'

Germany surrendered on 7 May 1945 and most German and other Axis POWs thought that they would be repatriated back to their homes in Europe, but this was not to be. Britain was desperate for labour after the war and with no further hold over the Italian POWs, now repatriated, the Germans were seen as an ideal replacement to fill this labour shortfall.[8] Some of the German POWs were held in Gloucester until the final camp closed on 28 March 1948. Those that were seen as essential labour in rebuilding Germany were more fortunate in acquiring earlier release to civilian status.

On 5 July 1945, Churchill lost the general election and Clement Attlee became the new Labour prime minister of Britain. Attlee made it clear to all the Axis partners that POWs were to help rebuild Britain, as it was their countrymen who had caused the destruction in the first place. Such was the need to rebuild Britain that Germans and others were also transported back to Britain from holding camps in Canada and the USA, as well as Belgium and other European countries. There are several accounts of German personnel being told in America that they were being repatriated home, only to find themselves arriving at the port in Liverpool. POWs were immediately put on trains to various parts of Britain, where some found themselves arriving at Moreton-in-Marsh, Gloucestershire.[9]

Following the Allied invasion of Europe in 1944 a large number of German POWs arrived from holding camps in France, Italy and Belgium. On arrival at British ports they, like the Italians before them, were firstly deloused and then taken by train to one of nine 'command cages'. Here the prisoners would be interrogated by army specialist officers, some of whom were Polish and fluent in the German language. Those considered to hold more important information were sent to special interrogation units where a number of methods were used to extract the information via hidden microphones, sleep deprivation or undercover informers.

One important task in this interrogation was to establish the degree of loyalty the prisoner had for the Nazi regime. The POWs were then graded as to their Nazi sympathies and issued with a coloured patch that was to be worn on their uniform: white or category 'A' for those with little loyalty to National Socialism and not seen as a security threat; grey or category 'B' for those that had no great feelings either way; and finally black or category 'C' for supporters of the Nazi philosophy or members of the Waffen SS. Efforts were made, sometimes without success, to keep the ardent followers apart from those that had no strong political views.

THE POW CAMPS OF GLOUCESTERSHIRE

The POW camps within the county developed primarily with the compulsory requisition by the War Office of land on which to build them, or the re-use of existing army and air force accommodation. Some large properties were also requisitioned such as Quedgeley Court, Swindon Manor Estate and Leckhampton Court.

America entered the war in December 1941 and many new army camps were built to accommodate the vast number of American 'GIs' arriving in the UK. Gloucestershire received many thousands of these troops in places such as Tewkesbury, Daglingworth, Cheltenham and the north Cotswolds, and all these troops and support staff had to be housed. Many logistical bases were set up in preparation for the D-Day landings on 6 June 1944, with units based in and around Moreton-in-Marsh, Blockley and Northwick Park. Some of these camps were later utilised as POW camps, after being vacated by the American forces.

In addition to the 'GI' accommodation, the Americans also built military hospitals in and around Gloucestershire, with one at Northwick Park eventually being re-designated by the International Red Cross as a hospital for German casualties only.

Other smaller hostels were built by the Ministry of Agriculture, Fisheries & Food just prior to the war in order to accommodate agricultural workers, but they were used instead to house small numbers of POWs. Some of these hostels were greatly enlarged.

The Geneva Convention allowed for the POWs to undertake work of a non-military nature only. Officers were exempt from working but other ranks were often grateful for work, reporting that it alleviated the boredom and waiting that was experienced during confinement in a POW camp. Prisoners would usually be detailed to do farm work, which would involve hedging, ditching and harvesting, or construction work. They were later employed at some RAF stations in the county. If working on farms, they would be under the direct command of the farmer by whom they were employed. POWs housed at farms were to have the same accommodation expected by a British soldier, such as a room, hot and cold water and a suitable bed. The prisoners undertaking this work received a wage initially paid into their account to spend at the camp shop.

After the German surrender, many Germans who had been tradesmen were used in the construction industry. The bombing campaign by the Germans meant that, after the war, there was a drastic housing crisis in Britain; it was estimated that some 4 million homes had been destroyed which would have to be replaced. Work and working conditions had generally to be approved by the trade unions, who were also concerned that troops returning to Britain and needing employment should be given priority.

Whilst work was essential in rebuilding Britain, the authorities quickly realised that Germany itself needed rebuilding – as well as re-educating away from the Nazi philosophy and towards a more democratic regime. Officers commanding prisoner-of-war camps were asked to appraise their captives to identify men who had provided essential services before the war, such as policemen, builders, miners etc. These men were given preferential treatment in repatriation.

Camp 37

Sudeley Castle, Winchcombe

Sudeley POW Camp 37 at Winchcombe SP 030 278, 9 May 1946.[1]

 THE ITALIANS

Camp 37 was first visited by Mr R. Haccius on behalf of the International Committee of the Red Cross (ICRC) on 23 July 1942.[2]

This camp, like many others, was built by the Italian POWs whilst under guard by the British Pioneer Corps. The Italian prisoners arrived in Winchcombe by train and were then marched to the site of the new camp within the grounds of the Sudeley Castle estate. Some of the British Pioneer Corps were housed at No. 62 Northgate Street, Winchcombe.[3]

The name of the camp commandant is not recorded in the first few reports but the Italian camp leader was Sergeant Major Giuseppe Furlanetto. There were 553 Italian POWs housed in the camp: one medical officer and 552 warrant officers and soldiers. The original ICRC reports were written in French but they are very comprehensive and give a good idea about the daily life of the prisoners and the conditions of their confinement.

Camp 37 was described as an agricultural camp of very recent construction. It was situated in the grounds of Sudeley Castle, which had been requisitioned by the War Office. Its location was described as a quiet area surrounded by hills, near the village of Winchcombe and approximately 12 miles from Cheltenham, and the climate was reported as 'healthy'.

The inspector found that the new huts were roomy and described them as of three types: Nissen, reinforced concrete and Tarrant huts. All were double walled and well insulated from the ground and each contained two air-heaters for warmth in winter. Three huts were reserved as meeting rooms and a dining room. The ration of coal in the camp was fixed at 20lb per man per day in summer and 56lb in winter, which was sufficient to maintain a suitable temperature in each hut. The maximum capacity of Camp 37 was set at 600 men, with each hut capable of housing up to forty prisoners. (There was, however, no mention that some POWs were still housed under canvas as the camp was not fully completed at this time.)

The interior installation consisted of bunk beds made out of wood with metal grids, straw mattresses or palliasses, and the prisoners were provided with three blankets in summer and four in winter. The lighting and ventilation was said to be sufficient and all the huts were lit by electricity. The provision of fire protection was applied according to the army regulations for such camps. From other camp reports this fire protection was usually two buckets of sand inside the hut and one bucket of water outside.

A local farmer recalls that there were problems constructing the water tower but that this was eventually overcome, resulting in adequate water at a suitable pressure for the sanitary facilities. There were twenty-four flushing toilets, and ten showers with a hot water supply, but this was found to be insufficient and further toilets and showers had to be constructed.

The rations complied with the recommendations of the Geneva Convention for POWs and they were inspected daily by the camp leader. The menu for the week was established by the chef and on the day of the ICRC visit was as follows:

Breakfast: Milk, coffee, margarine, marmalade and bread
Lunch: Soup, fried potatoes, greens and minced beef
Supper: Soup, cooked bacon, bread, milk and coffee

The British authorities at this time did not understand the cultural differences in dietary requirements for their newly established prisoners, but after general complaints from this and other POW camps the diet was changed, as far as was possible, to a more continental diet. Whilst it is not mentioned for Camp 37, later reports from other camps in Gloucestershire stated that they had acquired a hut for making macaroni.

> The British discovered that the Italians preferred more bread and less meat. They liked a loose loaf rather than the denser tinned loaf, vegetable soup and macaroni as much as possible. Quantity rather than quality. One War Office official requested that a more liberal diet of bread and vegetable soup be provided arguing that it would prove cheaper than the 'depot diet' laid down by the military authorities.[4]

The infirmary was installed in one of the Nissen huts and any POW in a serious condition was generally evacuated to the nearest civilian hospital. One case of tuberculosis was evacuated to a hospital in Oxford.

The POWs all wore their battledress, which was replaced or repaired by the camp tailors when necessary. The camp leader and the medical officer, both of whom were protected personnel, wore their full uniforms. Underclothing and toilet articles were given to each Italian POW on arrival in England at their reception camp. They each received one 112g bar of soap per week, which they considered to be an insufficient quantity.

The prisoners were paid for their work in accordance with the Geneva Convention, though officers did not have to work. The pay was 1s (5p) per day for the qualified workmen and 6d (2½p) per day for the labourers. The pay for warrant officers was 2s (10p) per week, and for warrant officers below the rank of adjutant and for regular soldiers the pay was regularly reviewed. Prisoners were not allowed to have actual money and would be disciplined if found to be in possession of any, but they were issued with tokens that could be exchanged for goods in the camp canteen. Other moneys earned were deposited in the prisoner's personal account to be handed over when repatriated.

The working hours were limited to eight hours per day. The POWs were transported to their work either by the army authorities of the camp, or by the farmers themselves. It is recorded that 439 men were at work or otherwise occupied on the day of the ICRC visit:

253 doing agricultural work (lodging at the camp)
 50 doing agricultural work (lodging at hostels)
 19 doing agricultural work (lodging in billets on the farms)
117 foresters (lodging at the camp)

The remainder were occupied at work, servicing or running the camp.

The POWs enjoyed a large amount of liberty during their work. Those who were questioned during the inspection declared that they preferred the distraction that occupation brought to them rather than the otherwise monotonous life in the camp.

The inspector found that the canteen was well provisioned, and the profits were used for the purchase of books, plays, seeds, sheet music and articles for sport. The turnover for June 1942 reached £460. He noticed, when examining the accounts, that a collection had been made by the inhabitants of Winchcombe for the following Christmas. This had raised the sum of £21 11s 6d (£21 58p) to improve the funds of the canteen.

Most of the Italian prisoners were Roman Catholics and a Catholic Mass was celebrated each week by Father Francis P. Ryan from Winchcombe. The diary of the Catholic bishop, the Rt Revd William Lee, indicated that he celebrated Mass with the prisoners on several occasions: once to conduct a Confirmation on 8 March 1943 and again to take Mass on Saturday, 17 April 1943.[5] The local farmers going to church on a Sunday morning would take along any Italian POW who wanted to attend a church service.

This camp offered excellent recreation facilities for the prisoners to enjoy in their leisure time, including billiards, table tennis and boccia. Football was practised on Sundays on the sports field in Winchcombe. Soon the POWs were playing football against the guards, other nearby POW camps, and even the village football team.

The inspector reported that the POWs had built a theatre complete with lighting and stage accessories and, to judge from some of the programs they had recently performed, he thought the men displayed a lot of talent.

Courses of study and in particular the English language were organised by the POWs. The books regularly received from the International Red Cross gave them a lot of pleasure. The choice was good and the subjects were varied, though it must be realised that the books supplied were subject to censorship. Books of study and techniques concerning agriculture were requested by the prisoners. A radio was provided for them and speakers were placed as high as possible within the camp. Permission was given for them to listen to the Italian station and certain programmes from Radio Roma.

The mail from Italy arrived at regular intervals, with the letters taking approximately four weeks to reach their destination. The prisoners could send a letter and a card each week. Letters addressed to the delegation of the Committee of the International Red Cross, London, or to the Italian Red Cross, were not limited. Some packets were sent by the Italian Red Cross to the camp after two POWs, whose names had been sent to Geneva, complained that they had not received any news of their families.

HOSTELS MANAGED BY CAMP 37

The inspector visited one of two hostels dependent on the camp that were approximately 7 miles away. These 'hostels' were built at the beginning of hostilities by the Ministry of Agriculture in order for future workers to be closer to the work deemed necessary for the planned intensive agricultural production programme. The hostels were very comfortable and particularly well equipped with showers and sanitary facilities. Their maximum capacity was approximately 100 men. There was no wire enclosure and one British sergeant was responsible for good order and discipline within these hostels.

The two hostels were not named in the report but it is quite possible that one was at Newtown near Ashchurch, Tewkesbury. Today this is the site of the Canterbury Leys public house, Ashchurch Road, Tewkesbury.

LOCAL FARM BILLETS

The inspector requested authorisation to visit some local farms where Italian POWs were billeted. These farms are not named in the report.

He reported that the POWs on the farm visited had good lodgings, two or three prisoners per room, having beds and hand-washing basins. They ate in the kitchen, reported that they were satisfied with the food, and could circulate freely within a radius of 1 mile from the farm. Many commanders of POW camps were of the opinion that, insofar as it did not result in any difficulties for the family they were billeted with, it would be possible to place a greater number of POWs in the farms or staying on the same site as their work as a matter of policy.

Sergeant Major Furlanetto was the camp leader at Sudeley: he was described as an able and conscientious man who enjoyed the full confidence of his fellow compatriots. He estimated that, as far as circumstances allowed, the commander and the administration of the camp did all that was in their capacity to make bearable the fate of the POWs. He made the following requests of the ICRC inspector:

1 He asked for a specimen of the Convention of 1929 relative to treatment to prisoners of war sent in the Italian language (a requirement of the Convention)
2 The camp leader wished to ensure a vegetable reserve for winter and request that one allocates an allotment out of the confines of the camp
3 He hoped that the few prisoners of war still under the tents would be transferred into the huts very soon
4 The camp orchestra would like musical instruments
5 The prisoners of war staying in hostels demand that the 3-valve radios are replaced by 5-valve models that are able to receive Radio Roma

The conclusions of Mr R. Haccius's report:

> The general impression taken during the visit was that it was excellent. The spirit of co-operation between the Administration of the Camp and the prisoners was obvious.
>
> The question by Camp Leader (No.2 above) would deserve to be examined generally for all the Camps. The Delegate sees a need of ensuring in winter the green vegetable supply essential to the maintenance of the current good state of health.

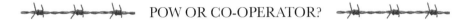 POW OR CO-OPERATOR?

With the dismissal of Mussolini on 25 July 1943 it was becoming obvious that the Italian Government was on the point of surrendering to the Allies. Concern was expressed by the War Office about the estimated 75,000 British and American prisoners held by the Italians. Arrangements were under way for some form of prisoner exchange but, before this could take place, many prisoners held by the Italians were taken by the Germans and transferred to more secure German POW and even concentration camps (in contravention of the Geneva Convention).

Italy surrendered on 8 September 1943 and the Italian Government, led by Badoglio, made very little progress regarding prisoner exchanges. The Badoglio regime was granted the status of 'co-belligerent', rather than be seen now as an 'ally', for a number of political reasons.

The reader can imagine the excitement of the POWs in Britain at the prospect of returning to their homeland. However, it was not to be. Britain needed their labour for the war effort and needed them to remain prisoners for disciplinary and management reasons. Eventually a compromise was agreed but never politically ratified, namely that the Italian POWs held here could volunteer as co-operators with the war effort and in return they would have extra privileges and conditions. Those who refused would be sent to secure POW camps until the war with Germany and Japan was finally over. The vast majority chose to stay and to continue working on farms, roads and in forest work.

Between the end of 1943 and 3 December 1944, the Italian soldiers at Sudeley were moved to better quarters and farm billets until their eventual repatriation. In the case of Sudeley, the recently vacated United States Army camp at the top of Broad Meadows Road in Winchcombe was used to rehouse many of the Italians. (This was a Nissen-hutted camp in a field above Nos 20 and 15 Broad Meadows Road.)

 PERSONAL RECOLLECTIONS

Personal recollections received from some Winchcombe residents relating to the Italian prisoners of war:

It was not long before the Italians were allowed out on their own without escort to the great delight of some of the local girls.

Ian Frances

Something very memorable happened to me as I walked back from Winchcombe one afternoon. An Italian prisoner of war was sitting on the parapet of the bridge over the river Isbourne and he started to speak to me. I think it was the first time I had ever spoken to a foreigner and I was distinctly nervous, especially as he was one of the enemy. He said he was trying to improve his English so could I try and teach him the words of a popular song, 'Marezeedotes an dozeedotes an liddlamzeedivy, a kidleedivytoo, wouldn't you?' ('Mares eat oats and does eat oats and little lambs eat ivy, a kid'll eat ivy too, wouldn't you?') … He then thanked me and gave me a cigarette, my first ever.

Alan Tompsett

I distinctly remember one Italian, who we were led to believe was a hermit in Italy before being recruited. He was quite an expert in producing meals from natural sources but his stews and hotpots were too hotly spiced for us Englanders.

Len Willett

 THE AUSTRIANS AT SUDELEY

The first of the Austrian prisoners of war arrived at Sudeley Camp 37 on 3 December 1944.

Hitler's life-long ambition was to return Austria to the 'Greater German Reich' and when his troops marched into Austria in 1938 the world saw pictures of an ecstatic dictator with what appeared to be the vast majority of Austrians cheering his arrival.

It is a matter of debate now as to how much support Hitler actually received from the Austrians but, at a meeting of the Allies in Moscow in October 1943, it was decided that after Germany's defeat Austria should be re-established as an independent entity. Austria was reclassified as Hitler's first victim in the conflict, a view still somewhat controversial given the help offered to Hitler in his plans for world domination. As there was some hostility between these two Axis partners, the German and Austrian POWs were generally kept apart if at all possible. Austria was occupied by the Four Powers of Occupation until the State Treaty of 1955.

The POW camps in Britain were now inspected by both the ICRC and the COGA (Control Office for Germany and Austria and Foreign Office, German Section). The COGA inspectors' role was to inspect the camps with a view to the education of the prisoners about democracy and related political ideology. They were responsible for providing lecturers and the production of exhibitions, films and publications. They also managed any dealings with the press and other interested agencies.

Dr Mamie inspected the camp on behalf of the ICRC on 20 July 1945.[6]

The camp commandant was named as Major A. Harris and his adjutant was Captain D. Lapscomb. The camp capacity was given as 1,025 and the total strength on the day of the inspection was 1,022 prisoners in the main camp with a further sixty-six in a hostel, a total of 1,088; all were Austrians. The Camp Leader was Wilhelm Kohla, No. 444624, and his rank was given as 'Stabsfeldwebel' (a warrant officer class 2 British equivalent or a master sergeant in the United States Army). The hostel was said to be able to house a maximum of seventy men and the camp leader had permission to visit the hostel whenever he so wanted.

Between the different barracks concrete paths, flowerbeds and lawns make a very pleasant impression. On one side of the enclosure there is a big kitchen garden and at one end a spacious sports field.

Mention is made by the inspector that a new rations scale was in use but that it was 'not quite satisfactory' for the hard workers and men spending the whole day in the open. The commandant was aware of this problem and told the inspector that 'the quality of the work and its efficiency have certainly decreased in the last two months, and that this is not due to any bad will on the POWs' part'.

With the money from the Welfare Fund the camp leader was able to purchase some bread and vegetables from local sources, which were then distributed as supplementary rations. The food was prepared in two well-equipped kitchens by Austrian cooks who provided three meals a day, the midday meal being cold but with hot tea or coffee.

The Italians had left a well-equipped infirmary with a patient room, isolation room, dispensary, pharmacy and a special dental department. The Austrians made good use of these facilities, with two NCOs who were qualified doctors and seven orderlies who gave medical treatment. Dental care was carried out by a British dentist who came twice a week.

Dr Mamie of the ICRC reported that on the day of his visit there were four men in the infirmary suffering from minor ailments. Those with more serious diseases were evacuated to a neighbouring military hospital.

The report goes on to claim that 'The personal property of some of the POWs has been taken away from them in various transit camps. Nothing has been taken in this camp.' This will be discussed further, as several ICRC reports highlight this loss of personal property and it was to become of great concern and unrest to some prisoners in other Gloucestershire POW camps.

The POWs were employed primarily in agricultural work and drainage, and 150 were working as woodsmen. They left the camp at 7.30 a.m. and returned between 5.30 p.m. and 7 p.m., working an eight-hour day and forty-eight-hour week. The prisoners worked in detachments of ten to twelve personnel under the supervision of their squad leaders. They were allowed free time on Saturday afternoons and Sundays. Those working in the camp (seventy men) took walks of up to two and a half hours every Sunday. Several instructors carried out the physical training; there was also football, handball, light athletics, gymnastics and boxing.

The report of the ICRC gives an extensive list of books and journals that were available in the camp library. There were fourteen schoolteachers amongst the POWs and they had organised the following studies: English for beginners, English for the advanced, shorthand and finally German language, literature, history and geography.

Every man in the camp was issued with fifty cigarettes and ¼ litre of beer (½ pint) every week. Toilet articles and razor blades were available to the men but the report states that 'sweets are no longer available'. Many items could be purchased from the camp canteen by which the POWs could supplement their rations.

The majority of the POWs, some 933, were reported to be Roman Catholics, with a further thirty-six Protestants. For the Italians a local Catholic priest had said Mass every Sunday but now, due to the high numbers involved, he had to say Mass three times each Sunday. The report then says, 'The RC Priest Fr Francis P. Ryan at Winchcombe does not appear to be ideal.' No explanation is given for this opinion.

The prisoners organised a small orchestra of thirteen men and they possessed between them: six violins, one cello, one double bass, one trumpet, one clarinet, one piano, one accordion and one set of percussion instruments. All of these instruments were purchased by the camp commandant and paid for from the camp welfare fund, which stood at £100 when Dr Mamie visited. This orchestra gave concerts of light and classical music and was most popular amongst the POWs. In addition to the orchestra there was a theatre company of fifteen to twenty men who gave performances every fortnight, and the orchestra's conductor had written many plays for this company.

Further entertainment was provided by wireless sets that were installed in several of the camp barracks. The camp had a cinema where films were shown every Saturday, including news of the week and educational films, also some German films lent by the local YMCA.

English newspapers and *Die Wochenpost* were supplied to the POWs on a regular basis and the ICRC report lists German, Swiss and Austrian newspapers but indicates that their delivery was sporadic.

The inspectors reported that the POWs were experiencing very poor communications with their friends and families. Very few letters or parcels were delivered to the camp and the ICRC promised to try to reorganise the system then in place and provide a better service.

Whilst the men made no complaints to the inspector, they did make one request. The inspector wrote: 'Once a detachment of Austrian POWs were working on the same farm as a German detachment; the Camp Leader has asked that such contacts be avoided. The Commandant agreed with the request.'[7]

The report described the discipline at the camp as 'excellent'. The Austrian POWs had been policing the camp themselves. They concluded that it was an excellent camp with the best co-operation between the commandant and the prisoners. It was said to be very well organised by an active and intelligent camp leader.

Captain Alexander, a COGA inspector, visited the camp several times between 2 October 1945 and mid-1946. His reports refer to the ICRC visits but he does ask the commandant to provide more political lectures.

By 15 January 1946 the camp numbers had increased to 1,261 and there were now five hostels administered by Camp 37. There were 705 men at the main camp in Sudeley Castle with a further fifty-two at Alderton, 240 at Moreton-in-Marsh, sixty-five at Newtown, fifty-one at Sezincote and fifty-one at Stanton. There were also ninety-seven POWs billeted on local farms.

Major Cormac of the British Pioneer Corps became the new camp commandant on 21 June 1946 and the report states that two POW teachers from Camp 181 (Springhill) were transferred to Sudeley to support the educational programme.

On 10 February 1946 the camp had a visiting lecturer, Miss A. Kaldegg, who gave a talk on 'Advertising and Propaganda'. This was well received by the POWs and her appraisal report quotes several prisoner questions, one of which was: 'If this is a democratic country, why is it that a prisoner has no right against an employer who strikes him?' While another POW asked, 'Why aren't we allowed to talk to British people?'

Other lectures include one by Dr Walter Viiman in April entitled 'The Social Order of Democracy'. This was met by a degree of cynicism and complaints that it was far too long. His expenses were 14s 3d (71p) for his train journey from Birmingham and 3s 6d (18p) for tea at Cheltenham. Another speaker, E.F. Stark, got a very good report from the POWs for his talk on 'Democracy and Fascism'. This talk was relayed by loudspeaker to all barrack rooms so that the entire camp could hear it.[8]

The camp was then inspected by Dr E.H. Strehler on behalf of the ICRC on 21 February 1946, just a few weeks before the Austrian POWs were repatriated to Europe, the last of whom left on 19 May 1946.[9]

By February many of the Austrians had been moved to transit camps ready to be repatriated and only 883 remained: one officer, ninety-one NCOs and 791 men. The camp leader remained, Wilhelm Kohla, but the commandant was now Major S.G. Graham.

The report on the infirmary gives the name of the medical officer as Oberarzt Josef Hnilicka, A775066, a category 'A' prisoner. One death was recorded since the previous report: Josef Raab, 91961, died on 8 January in Chepstow hospital with cerebral tumours and was buried with military honours at Chepstow.[10]

A short two-page report contains the following questions that the Austrian POWs wanted to ask the delegate:

1   Why was there no correspondence?
2   Why were protected personnel (PP) not recognised?
3   Why were Austrian POWs not given a nationality tab like the Italians?
4   Why were they not allowed to get in touch with the Austrian ambassador?
5   Whether Austrians had any priority in repatriation?
6   Why POWs with bad news from their families were not allowed to go home and
    help them.

The inspector explained the fundamental paragraph of the Geneva Convention,
especially as to the question of repatriation.

Again the report concludes by saying how well the camp was run and ends with:
'The uncertainty about the Austrian POW political situation and its consequences
upon the Austrian POW may cause sometimes a certain depression.'[11]

THE GERMANS AT CAMP 37

The last of the Austrian POWs had left Sudeley by 19 May 1946 and the first intake
of 1,025 Germans from Camp 185 Springhill near Broadway arrived, with a second
intake of fifty men from Camp 157 at Bourton-on-the-Hill two days later.

Many of the German POWs were originally imprisoned in the USA and were told
that they were now on their way home but this, it seems, was mainly to gain their
co-operation, as to their surprise they were landed in Liverpool. Britain still needed
labour and the then prime minister, Mr Attlee, felt that the Germans should help
repair the damage done during the war. (*See* Joachim Schulze's account in Chapter 4)

Other Germans were transferred from US army captivity in Britain and a further 200
POWs were brought in from Belgian camps: these were young conscripts to the German
Waffen SS. The COGA report of 17/18 August 1946 makes it clear that there was a bitter
morale amongst the POWs due to prisoners being transferred from the USA, Germany and
Belgium, and partly due to the reduction in cigarette ration and lack of entertainment.[12]

The hostel at Alderton opened in June 1946 and received seventy Germans,
the hostel at Newtown sixty-five, at Sezincote sixty, and at Stanton seventy-five
POWs, all under the administration of Camp 142 located in Brockworth, Gloucester.

Lectures continued during this period with subjects such as the Totalitarian State
and European Concept of Life; Germany Today, Yesterday and Tomorrow; Questions
on Democracy; British Parliament Institutions; International Relations and a new
political party system in Germany.[13]

Mr E.F. Peeler made an inspection of the camp on 27/29 October 1946 on behalf
of the COGA. The commandant was now Lt Col Hayward-Brown and the total
population was 1,366 POWs comprising 833 in the main camp, 444 in hostels and
eighty-nine billeted on farms.

The report looks at the educational programme and identifies two German teachers at the Moreton-in-Marsh hostel. There were regular talks at Alderton Hostel by a Revd Davis and at Newtown by the Revd Small of Tewkesbury. Alderton Hostel was almost empty now with just eight POWs. Mr Alfred Alexander gave a lecture on 16 May 1947, the subject being 'Civic rights in England and Germany'. Two lectures were given in the main camp and two of the hostels.

The number of POWs repatriated to date was given as 350.

Sudeley Camp 37 was inspected by Dr M. de Bondeli and Mr E.A. Aeberhard on 28 May 1947 for the ICRC.[14] It was also inspected by Mr A.T. Duff on 28/29 May on behalf of the COGA.[15]

The camp commandant was now Major F.S. Eaton and the camp strength was given as 656 men: 484 in the main camp, sixty-two at Stanton Hostel and a further 110 billeted. Of this number there were two officers and 654 NCOs, thirteen being recognised as PPs. Whilst the majority (628) of POWs were German, there were four Czechoslovakians and twenty-four Yugoslavians. This latter group had made application to the authorities for repatriation to Austria.

POW administration was now listed as:

Camp Leader: Fw. Anton ERDLE B38281. A native of Augsburg. He was described as a 'Good Type', a Roman Catholic, and a previous Hostel Leader who took over the main camp 3 weeks ago on the repatriation of the former Camp Leader.
Asst Camp Leader: O/Fw. Stevermann WITT B639818. A 31-year-old professional soldier since 1934.
Senior Medical Officer: Stabsarzt Hans BREME B689373, age 32, a professional soldier since 1932.
Protestant Chaplain: Lt Helmut DIETERICH A853214. A 30-year-old school teacher in 1938, a native of Wittenburg. Transferred from Camp 174 (Norton Camp, Mansfield, Notts).
Roman Catholic Chaplain (now) comes from Springhill Camp 185.

The report follows the usual format but the only changes noted were: 'Shortage of underwear and socks. Priority is given to POWs who are to be repatriated soon.' The theme is repatriation as it is noted that the orchestra has twelve instruments but only five musicians remain.

Dr Weber, a Swiss lecturer, was asked not to attend again as his lecture was 'Not a great Success'. The re-education activities included a camp newspaper, *Skizzen der Zeit* (*Sketches of the Time*), political discussion groups and an information room where three exhibitions were set up.

A small number from the main camp attended a meeting of the Cheltenham Town Council in May and a second group were to attend in June. One hundred POWs visited the Bath and West Agricultural Show at Cheltenham and visits were

arranged to Cheltenham Art Gallery, Museum and Library. Also reported was a visit
to Gloucester Cathedral.

In relation to work: apart from farm work, it now included fifteen men on road repairs.

By August 1947 the population of Sudeley Camp 37 was 750, with sixty at Sezincote,
seventy at Alderton, and seventy-five at Stanton Hostel. Moreton-in-Marsh Hostel,
known in some reports as Universal Hostel after Universal Farm, had 240 POWs.
Newtown Hostel closed on 20 March 1947 following local flooding.

MORETON-IN-MARSH (UNIVERSAL) HOSTEL

The three ICRC reports relating to Camp 37 at Sudeley make no mention of the
hostel at Moreton-in-Marsh. However, the COGA inspector, Captain Alexander,
does record that when he visited the Universal Hostel during his inspection of
Sudeley in October 1945 there were a total of 240 Austrian POWs.

The first group of 201 German POWs arrived in Moreton-in-Marsh on 28 April 1946
and were accommodated at Universal Hostel; as the Austrians were yet to leave the main
camp at Sudeley it would appear that the Austrians were no longer at the hostel. Of the
201 Germans, fifty were from the USA, 150 from BAOR in Belgium, and one German
was included following his attendance on the training he received at Wilton Park.

The report states that most of the Germans had been recruited to the German Army
from reserved occupations or as very young conscripts to the Waffen SS, and had been
called up because of the need to increase the number of soldiers. They were classified
upon arrival as being 70 per cent Black (category C) and 30 per cent Grey (category
B); of these soldiers forty-five were under the age of 25 years.

The hostel leader was named as S/Fw. Karl Bruemann, a 45-year-old civil servant
who had worked in the German Post Office since 1930. He had been a party member
since 1932 and the inspector reported that he was 'An opportunist of poor character
and graded as B-'.

The German police chief was Fw. Adolf Braun, a 31-year-old bookkeeper and said
to be non-political. He was Polish by birth and was also graded as B.

The COGA report of 2 October 1946 states that the hostel was now made up
almost entirely of Waffen SS. All were under the supervision of a British staff sergeant
of the Pioneer Corps. The highest number of POWs recorded at Moreton-in-Marsh,
Universal Hostel, was given as 300 men in October 1946. This was the last report to
include the hostel and it would appear to have closed shortly afterwards as it is not
mentioned in the COGA report for Sudeley on 28 May 1947.

There was a tragic incident at Universal Hostel in October 1946, which has been
recorded in full detail. The following report is included with the permission of the
Gloucestershire coroner concerning the suicide of Ewald Issel A725786 Waffen SS at
Moreton-in-Marsh Hostel.[16]

Ewald Issel was born on 15th April 1908 at Altenderne, Luenennord Germany, and died of his own hand on Wednesday 16th October 1946 aged 38 and 6 months.

Before the war Ewald was a painter by profession and became a voluntary member of the German Security Police before eventually drifting into the Waffen SS serving as a U/Scha [L/Cpl] Unterscharführer, a junior squad leader and paramilitary rank of the Nazi Party as used by the Schutzstaffel [SS] between 1934 and 1945.

He was captured at Holstein, Germany, on 2nd May 1945. Since his capture he was held at the following POW Cages, Holstein 3rd May 1945 to 11th June 1945, and Neuengame 11th June 1945 to 31st October 1945.

He was then transferred to England on 15th April 1946, arriving on 18th April 1946 at Camp 185 Springhill.

Posted to Camp 37 Sudeley Castle on 29th April 1946 where he was sent to Universal Hostel in Moreton-in-Marsh he was employed on agricultural work with Mr Butler of Upper Slaughter nr Cheltenham and was so employed on the day of his death.

He returned to camp with the other POWs at the usual time of 6pm on the 16th October and once free of the roll call he and the other prisoners were free to roam the camp.

At 9.55pm Gerhard Gatter B204771 had need to visit the incinerator where he found Ewald hanging from a beam. He was cut down and carried to the sick quarters and the NCO, Staff Sergeant Sykes of the Pioneer Corps, was notified. The NCO then rang for Dr. Schiller at Bengal House, Moreton-in-Marsh.
Adolph Braun A797533, a POW at Universal Hostel, said his job was to check POWs back into camp and to report any that were missing. At 6 p.m. he checked the lorry bringing men back from the Upper Slaughter route and all were present.

At 7 p.m. Adolph told Ewald to get ready for an investigation as to his political views so that he could be classified for his repatriation. There was a lecture on repatriation that evening in the camp that finished at 9.45 p.m. and several witnesses at the enquiry thought that Ewald had attended.

Gerhard Gatter worked as a staff clerk in the German Office at the hostel and having found Ewald said he called for the medical orderly from the hospital and also reported the incident to the camp sergeant, Otto Hubscher A992114.

Thomas Gullan, a police constable at Moreton-in-Marsh, was called to the hostel in Stow Road and met Staff Sergeant Sykes of the Pioneer Corps. He was the NCO in charge of the hostel and together they visited the brick-built incinerator building, which was situated on the south side of the hostel. Constable Gullan told the court that the underside of the beam from which Ewald had hung himself was just 6ft 3in from the ground and the deceased height was 5ft 11in. It appeared that Ewald had stood on tip-toe and then slumped. There was no sign of foul play.

Universal Hostel (1) SP 205 325 and Moreton-in-Marsh railway station (2), 27 May 1944.[17]

The *Citizen* newspaper reported the incident and said that the German POW had left behind him a wife and two children, one boy and one girl, back in Germany. It appears that Ewald was concerned that he would be sent back to Germany where he would be tried at Nuremburg as a member of the SS. A suicide note was found in his pocket that read:

> I cannot live any longer; I am spiritually and morally finished. The thought of my wife and children living in need and distress gives me no peace of mind. I was drafted into the SS [Waffen SS] through a dirty trick. I was a voluntary member of the security police. In my whole life I have never harmed anyone. I have a clear conscience.
>
> I have learned to hate the Nazis, who have brought suffering on myself and innumerable decent German people. Death is for me a release from this wicked world.

The note was signed by Ewald Issel.

 STANTON COURT HOSTEL

Stanton Court Hostel near Broadway was visited on 29 May 1947 by Mr E.A. Aeberhard, who reported:

1	Camp Leader:	B267816 Gefr Heinz SCHICK
2	In Charge:	Sgt. Mort.
3	Strength:	61 men.
4	Accommodation:	3 wooden barracks.
5	Sanitary Installations:	In Order.
6	Food:	'Gut' says Camp Leader.
7	Clothing:	Since March no exchanges.
8	Canteen:	Sufficient supply.
9	Labour:	Farm work.
10	Complaints:	None, except wish to receive clothing more regularly.
11	General Impression:	Good hostel. Morale is good among the young POWs. Elderly classes suffer from long captivity.[18]

THE END OF CAMP 37

Camp 37 at Sudeley Castle, Winchcombe, was later administered by Camp 185 Springhill some time between 6 June 1947 and November 1947. Finally it became a satellite camp under Leckhampton Camp 263. It closed on 20 January 1948 and, after housing the Land Army volunteers (slogan – 'Lend a Hand on the Land'), it was taken down. Today all that remains are the foundations to the footpaths that once ran in front of the huts.

3

Camp 61

Wynols Hill near Coleford, Forest of Dean
Camp 61 located at SO 586 106. 30 December 1946[1]

 THE ITALIANS

This POW camp was first visited by the International Committee of the Red Cross (ICRC) on 21 July 1942 when the main camp was in its early construction and not due for occupation until September. At the time of the visit by the ICRC inspector, Mr R.A. Haccius, the Italian prisoners were being housed in tents with eight men sleeping in each tent. They slept on wooden planks laid on the ground and each had three blankets. The tents did have electric lights. No mention is made of the facilities or the numbers of British personnel guarding these prisoners.[2]

Whilst the camp capacity is given as 750 men, there were 482 Italian POWs present at the time of his visit. This was to be a working camp and so there was only one Italian officer – medical officer, Dr Cavalli. The rest were made up of NCOs and other ranks (ORs).

The camp was built by the prisoners in a 384 x 580ft enclosure and the plans were for three types of huts: Nissen, concrete and plasterboard. There were to be twenty-one dormitories each housing forty men, three dining rooms, and four huts reserved as a hospital/infirmary. It was also intended to provide a meeting room for the prisoners. In addition to these huts, four concrete huts were to be built for the laundry, showers and toilets. Finally there were plans to provide a canteen, a kitchen, an office for the camp leader, and also workshops for the tailors and the shoemakers.

Not all of the prisoners were involved in the construction of Camp 61. At the time of the inspection 340 men were working in sawmills, with a further sixty men employed by the Forestry Commission felling oak trees. These prisoners were transported to their workplace by lorries and buses, leaving the camp at 7.30 a.m. and returning about 5 p.m.

The POWs received the regulation rations for outdoor agricultural work and on the day of the visit the menu consisted of:

Breakfast: Coffee, marmalade, margarine and bread
Lunch: Bread, milk, coffee and bacon
Supper: Macaroni, beefsteak, salad and bread

Those going out to work were issued with a cold lunch. The rations were received and controlled by camp leader, Sergeant Major Mario Piano, and his deputy.

The makeshift kitchens were well fitted and the camp leader informed the ICRC that the Italian cooks were satisfied with both the quantity and the quality of the food supplied by the British. It is noted here that generally the local population was not as well fed as the POWs. Under the Geneva Convention the prisoners were entitled to the same rations as their captors – in this case the British Army.

Ration scale for working Italian POW	Per day
Meat, fresh or frozen	4 oz
Margarine	1.5 oz
Bacon	1.28 oz
Bread (white or wheatmeal)	16 oz
Flour	1 oz
Rice	.43 oz
Cheese	1.14 oz
Cake	.57 oz
Jam	1 oz
Dried fruit	.85 oz
Coffee	1.5 oz
Sugar	2 oz
Milk, condensed	3 oz
Potatoes	16 oz
Fresh vegetables	5.72 oz
Dried vegetables	1.14 oz
Salt	0.37 oz
Cash allowance	1½ pence per day

Dr Cavalli and a British doctor visited the temporary infirmary on a daily basis and any patients who were in need of hospitalisation were transferred to a civilian hospital. Later reports indicate patients were sent to Gloucester Hospital and/or a military hospital in Chepstow. The 1942 report records one fatal accident when a prisoner fell from a lorry. His name is not recorded.

At this early stage of the war the Italian prisoners wore a dark brown battledress and changes to this uniform will be discussed later. Those prisoners working in the forest were issued with leather jackets or jerkins, which were to protect them from inclement weather. All POWs were issued with two sets of underclothes and socks, and they were provided with washing soap to use in the camp laundry or for personal hygiene.

The tented camp was supplied with a POW canteen and although it was well stocked it did not include items that were not available to the local people. The prisoners were allowed thirty-five cigarettes a week but they could purchase extra tobacco products on payment with their tokens. Twenty thousand cigarettes were sold in the canteen in the month of July and the visitors noted that the turnover was about £750 per month, a considerable sum. The profits made by selling items in the canteen went into a relief fund used to help prisoners in need or to purchase required equipment.

The British authorities were well aware that the prisoners were in need of leisure and intellectual activities and did their best to meet these needs. Both boxing and football were popular with the prisoners and a theatrical group had been set up, with productions given twice a month. The Italians requested a normal size football pitch as the one used was too small. Football was very popular to play or to watch and later they were allowed to play local teams. Listening to the radio was allowed by the authorities and loudspeakers were set up around the camp so that the radio could be played at certain times. Radio Roma was popular as were concerts of both popular and classical music.

Mr Haccius reported that the camp leader had the necessary authority and confidence of his compatriots and that the relationship between him and the commandant was very good. Sadly this was not to be the case in some other Gloucestershire camps.

By the time of the next inspection on 8 July 1943 by Messrs Müller and Célerier, the base camp was now in use although a few buildings were yet to be finished. The number of POWs was given as 825 and the camp capacity 950 men. There were in fact 580 POWs within the main camp and we are informed that the camp now had three additional hostels housing 144 men, with another 101 men living on farms around the area. These hostels are not named.[3]

The previous camp leader had resigned and the canteen manager was co-opted as camp leader on a temporary basis. He was Sergeant Major Becchi but he made it clear that he was not interested in taking on this role on a permanent basis.

The new camp dormitories were said to be light and airy with metal bunks. Heating was by two coal stoves and each hut had electric lighting. Prisoners were able to make additional furniture such as small tables, boxes and cases, which were interspersed between the bunks. Pictures and some drawings were pinned to the walls.

Each prisoner had a bedroll and four blankets and the visiting inspectors noted that the living accommodation was clean and well maintained. Fire protection was in the form of a foot pump and a bucket of sand inside the huts, with two buckets of water outside and near the entrance.

Two huts were set aside as toilet blocks with forty-eight flushing toilets and two 5m-long urinals. The toilet cubicles were built in two rows, back to back, and separated behind and on the lateral by brick walls giving the prisoners some degree of privacy.

Two identical huts provided shower, washing and laundry facilities. They each had twelve showers in open cubicles. Washing and laundry was done on long narrow tables about 10m long, which were placed under pipes from which hot and cold water could be obtained through seven taps. In each of these huts there was enough space so that fifty-six men could wash at the same time, as well as those who would be in the showers. The water was described as being very hot and the pressure good. The laundry was done by the POWs, who were provided with a monthly soap ration of 16oz, or 450g, for their washing and personal use.

The prisoners received the standard double supplies of clothing after some initial problems with their supply. The replacement of articles that were no longer usable was slow and repairs were done by the shoemakers and tailors who had their workshops in one of the huts, where a carpenter also worked. The ICRC inspectors reported that: 'It is to be noted that this carpenter and wood carver is a real artist and we admired some of his works.'[4]

The specialised workers were paid 1s (5p) a day, the others 6d (2.5p). In this camp only POWs who were permanently working on the upkeep of the camp or the hostels were recorded as non-specialised workers. Money earned was credited to their account and the same applies to the medical officer. Three hundred and sixty-six POWs were employed as agricultural labourers and a further 342 in the forests or in the sawmills. They worked a forty-eight-hour week on average. Some prisoners complained that the work in the sawmills was very tiring. Typical days started at reveille at 6.30 a.m., followed by breakfast and depart at 7.30 a.m. They returned around 5.30 p.m., then dinner from 6 p.m. and lights out at 10.30 p.m.

The POWs built a chapel in one of the refectories, which was used on Sundays with a local Catholic priest saying Mass; once a month a Catholic Silesian priest would visit the camp.

Many prisoners played sports during the afternoon with football being very popular. They had prepared a football pitch outside the camp but said it was barely usable, and they could only play football when they asked the commandant. Requests were made to see if a new pitch could be made within the camp setting but the aerial pictures of the camp, taken by the RAF, show that this did not happen. The POWs also had a volleyball court and a few areas for other ball games that were well laid out.

The prisoners that worked all week in the camp or hostels were allowed outside the camp for two periods of up to two hours each week, the others once for two hours on a Sunday. The medical officer, who was allowed to roam freely outside the camp as long as he promised (like everyone else) not to speak with anyone, refused to go out because of the great difficulty he would have in keeping his promise to the letter, especially if someone were to ask him a question.

This freedom to roam outside the camp may surprise the reader but medical officers were given protected personnel (PP) status under the Geneva Convention. In addition, the war with Italy was coming to an end with its surrender only two months away on 8 September 1943.

Other activities that were organised by the prisoners included an orchestra, and in one of the refectories they had constructed a theatre, which was apparently beautifully decorated. Evening classes built around the first three years of elementary education were organised and seventy pupils regularly attended these courses. The trainers who offered this education were an Italian sergeant and a soldier, who had both followed a period of instruction.

The inspectors reported that very few games were available and the prisoners really needed cards, draughts, chess and billiards. The YMCA organised film shows in most POW camps but these were not then available at Camp 61.

As far as correspondence was concerned, it was still very irregular with letters tending to take two months or more to arrive. With prisoners permitted to send a letter each week (specialist personnel were allowed to send twice as many) the lack of a quick reply did affect their morale and we will see later just how important letters were during the war.

Following the Italian surrender in September 1943, life changed for the Italian POWs. They were divided into co-operators and non-co-operators. Those that were willing to cooperate with the Allies and help the war effort were offered better conditions and more freedom of movement, whereas those who refused were sent to more secure POW camps. (*See* Chapter 5)

The deputy camp leader, Sergeant Major Bruno Porciani, is reported to have been involved in the design of both the camp chapel and the camp theatre. He is also credited with the construction of a very large monument dedicated to Guglielmo Marconi (1874–1937), who is famous as the father of long-distance radio transmission, radio telegraphy and Marconi's law.

The monument was started some time in 1944 and was made of concrete painted white so as to look like marble from a distance. It was reportedly built to commemorate the fiftieth anniversary of radio transmissions and was inaugurated on Christmas Day 1944. It was certainly a very large structure with a high central tower that could be climbed from the inside.

Shields showing the coats of arms of some Italian cities were placed on the two curtain walls, and the inscription in both Italian and English read: 'To Guglielmo Marconi. Magician of the ether. The Italian Prisoners of War.'

A local man remembers playing on the monument just before it was demolished. He recalls that by this time all the paintwork was gone and the two globes, Marconi bust and flagpole had disappeared; the structure had been vandalised and had become overgrown with dense brambles. He estimated the central column being about 12ft above the steps, with about 20ft between the globes.

Despite offers to repair and maintain the monument, including a donation from the Italian Government, the monument was demolished around 1961.[5]

 AN ITALIAN POW'S STORY

Andre (Andy) Russo was born on 20 April 1920 in Maddaloni, a small town or commune in the province of Caserta, and about 5km south-east of Caserta itself in Southern Italy. It is situated at the base of one of the Tifata hills, and with its medieval castle, the church of San Michele and overlooked by Mount Vesuvius, it is a very picturesque place. He was one of five boys all of whom served in the Italian Army; one brother was killed fighting on the Russian front.

Andre Russo, like many others, reported that he was pressed into the Italian Army by the Fascists, known as the Black Shirts, early in the Second World War.

Marconi Memorial Monument (Prot. N. 543/11). (Reproduced with kind permission of Radio Rivista, February 1995)[6]

The Black Shirts were so named because these armed squads of Italian Fascists under Benito Mussolini wore black shirts as part of their uniform. Russo fought as an infantryman in both Albania and then North Africa, where he was eventually captured like the thousands of others left stranded in the great Allied push in August 1942. He was captured by a Scottish regiment and he often told his family later that he and his comrades regretted being caught by the 'men in skirts' because they played 'Russian roulette' each night with the POWs. His daughter, Marilyn Champion, remembers him saying that his captors were 'often drunk each night on whisky and very barbaric'.

Marilyn says that her father recalled that generally he and his comrades were glad to be captured: they had no food, ammunition or fuel left and lived on snakes and other creepy-crawlies that they came across in the desert. He told her that they were at their lowest point. Certainly the records show that the

The photograph of Andre Russo shows him in the co-operator's uniform. It was a chocolate-brown battledress with shoulder flashes that read 'Italian'. The inverted chevrons worn on the left sleeve were good conduct badges, which were each issued after six months of trouble-free working. He is wearing three, which was the maximum allowable and they could be taken away as part of any disciplinary problems.[7]

captives were in a terrible state, suffering from dehydration, infestation and starvation. Andre Russo's army records are no longer available, but we have a very good idea as to what then happened to him.

At first he would have been transported or marched to a processing centre by his British captors in what were known as holding pens or cages. Here he would have been searched, deloused and treated medically for any illness or disease before then being questioned. When shipping transport became available he would have to board a ship full of fellow Italians destined, in his case, for a British port. These POW ships were as liable as any other Allied shipping to be sunk by the German Navy.

Andre later told his family that he and his comrades were badly received when they disembarked in Liverpool, which was possibly due to the fact that the local citizens were being heavily bombed by the Germans at this time. Liverpool had a large reception camp where prisoners were again assessed for suitability to work and then transferred to a designated POW camp. Andre was sent to Camp 61 at Wynols Hill near Coleford. Very few officers were sent to Britain as they did not have to work under the Geneva Convention and were sent to India or Canada.

Marilyn recalls her father saying that initially they were supervised but latterly they were not.

'I think they were all well behaved – and even chased the local ladies! I know they had a football team and they would play against the guards: Italy v England.'

Newent area
showing location
of POW hostel,
28 May 1947.[8]

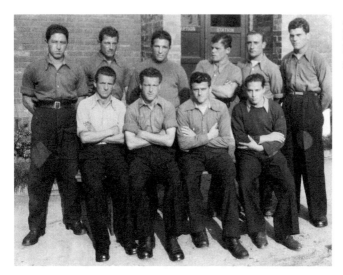

Andre Russo with his working group at Newent (back row, second from right).

Andre was later transferred to a small hostel in Newent where he joined a working party of ten fellow prisoners.

> Dad said they were well treated by the English and they became friendly with the farmers that they worked for on the land. He later gained his good conduct chevrons and was given agricultural work at Taynton and then Boulsdon farm, where he was to meet his future wife.

Following his repatriation to Italy in 1946 he, like so many others, came back to Britain; he returned to Gloucestershire where he later married his sweetheart at St Peters church in Gloucester. He became part of the Newent community and was to help build the Catholic church, Our Lady of Lourdes. He died on 14 January 1994.

Throughout his life Andre never forgave the Scottish soldiers who captured him but came to respect his English guards and experiences in Gloucestershire during his captivity. Life in Blighty, he told his family, was good to him and that is why he spent his life in Gloucestershire. In all, three of the Newent Hostel POWs returned to live in Newent and all were respected members of their community.

 THE GERMANS ARRIVE

As the last of the Italian Co-operators were being transferred before repatriation, the Germans arrived in two groups: one group of 120 men were due on 11 May, with the second group due in early June 1946. Both Germans and Italians were at the camp together for a few weeks, but no mention is made of how well this went with both the prisoners and the guards.

The German strength was made up as follows: Main Camp 120, Llanclowdy Hostel ninety-five, Drill Hall Hostel 164, Billettees twenty-five, making a total of 404 men including one officer.[9] The Italians that remained totalled 175: 174 men in the main camp including three sergeants, and one in Gloucester Prison. The last Italian camp leader was Sergeant Antonio Giangrandi 168924 and the camp commander was Major D. de B. Lipscombe. (Italians were repatriated after December 1946.)

The accommodation has been described above but information is given in the ICRC report of 16 June 1946 on two hostels. One hostel was near Ross-on-Wye, called Drill Hall. It was taken over a few weeks previously from Chepstow Camp 197 and was described as rather primitive. It consisted of fifteen old Nissen huts built in a meadow. The kitchen was reported as gloomy, with four brick walls covered with corrugated iron. Because of the camp's condition only one shower bath was permitted per week. The camp could accommodate up to 130 POWs and the original German arrivals came from another Gloucester camp, 157 at Springhill, on 12 March 1946.

The second hostel was at Llanclowdy and made a good impression on the inspecting officers. The report stated, however, that 'in this part of Britain they did not yet know what electricity was': both farmers and POWs used petrol lamps. The first POWs sent to Llanclowdy were from Camp 17, Lodge Moor Camp, Sheffield, Yorkshire.

Initially all German POWs were sent to work on farms and the farmers involved thought them better workers than the previous Italians. Until the end of 1944 employment of German POWs was not permitted but, with the Italians being repatriated, labour became a great issue. Twenty-five thousand German POWs under the control of the United States Army authorities in Britain were transferred to the British authorities, and the type of work permitted and the required numbers were discussed by the War Cabinet.

It would appear from the inspection notes that much of the recreational material used by the Italians was not available to the incoming Germans. No books, newspapers or musical instruments remained in the camp and no footballs. The Germans, however, were well organised and quickly arranged lessons and started several activities including a theatre group. Newspapers were obtained from the British staff after their use and others from local farmers. A radio was lent on a temporary basis to the Ross Hostel by a local Catholic priest.[10] Correspondence was very poor, with thirty-seven out of 120 in the main camp having no news about their relatives or loved ones. There was also much anxiety for POWs who came from what was now Russian-occupied territory.

There was an inspection on behalf of the COGA on 19 November 1946 by Mr Gibson. Major D. de B. Lipscombe had been replaced by Lt Col Moreton as camp commander. The main objective was to look at prisoner re-education in their political views and indoctrination. The POWs were offered lectures, films and visits to museums, council meetings and other public events. Mr Gibson made a scathing report on a staff sergeant because he gave no encouragement for re-education, was negligent and a hindrance to the re-education programme.[11]

The inspector included a report on a popular Roman Catholic priest who visited Highnam Court Hostel. Apparently he was made welcome by the Germans as he was fluent in their language. On 15 May 1947 the camp commander was Major Caynton, and the camp numbers were still increasing – now 1,101 POWs. There was a report of one escapee. When recaptured, the offence of escaping usually incurred a sentence of twenty-eight days' confinement.

The morale of the POWs was very poor at this time for a number of reasons. These included re-screening with the result that a lot of prisoners saw their assessment grade of 'C' being raised to 'D', which would delay their repatriation. Another was the removal of the British quartermaster who got on well with the prisoners.

At Highnam Court Hostel there was discontent due to the arrival of sixty men from a camp where the food was said to be better and where any patched clothing was exchanged for new. The camp leader at this time was O/Gefr Werner Hausweiler, aged 29 and classified as 'B+'.

POWs were now allowed out of camp until 10 p.m. and many worked overtime to earn extra money for their eventual repatriation. This did not go down well with the inspector as it was seen as handicapping all camp re-education activities.

Prisoners now attended church services in Coleford town. There was also a camp magazine called *Die Bestimmung* (*Destiny*), published fortnightly.

The last ICRC visit took place on 7 July 1947 when the inspector was Dr G. Hoffmann. By this time all the Italian prisoners had been repatriated and the camp, with its hostels and billets, had a population of 1,075 men, of which ten were protected personnel. This number was made up of:

In Camp	456
Hostel 1. Highnam Court	296
Hostel 2. Ross	198
Hostel 3. Llanclowdy	63
Billets	62

POW Administration:

Camp Leader	Obermaat	Bruno Zauber A489542
Asst. Camp Leader	O/Fw.	Peter Becker A45780
Senior M.O.	Stabsarzt	Dr Rudolf Stiawa A963526
Protestant Chaplain	Fähnrich	Friedrich Schroeder A482589
Studienleiter	Soldat	Klaus Ingverson B44117
Dentist	Gefr	Oswald Winkler B177786

The German prisoners that arrived were made up of 25 per cent from the USA, 10 per cent from the Channel Islands, and the rest (65 per cent) from POW camps in

Germany. Their work involved about 60 per cent working in agriculture with the rest in quarries, sawmills and in forestry.

In addition to the usual information, the report did include several items of interest, including the fact that Highnam Court had eight beds in its infirmary, and two prisoners had been transferred to Camp 152 Bourton-on-the-Hill because of repeated attempts to escape.

Also highlighted was a report that:

> In this camp there exists a Camp Parliament. Every hut sends a representative to this parliament (elected by secret ballot). Meetings every month under the presidency of the Camp Leader. The two bigger Hostels have their own parliament. Every four weeks all the Hostel leaders have a meeting with the Main Camp Leader.

The overall impression reported by Dr G. Hoffmann was that the camp was very good, with excellent collaboration between the commandant and the camp leader in the general interest of the community. The morale in Camp 61 was given as higher than in the average camp.[12]

Of the hostels, his report concluded that the Drill Hall Hostel (Ross), previously reported as primitive, was now in good condition, also that Llanclowdy was still without electricity and there was no sign of any change. The Llanclowdy Hostel Leader was Maat Frazer Maltus 'B+' and the report stated that the camp was soon to be closed and the prisoners transferred. The assistant camp leader was promoted to camp leader at the end of July. O/Fw. Peter B. Becker was a 33-year-old professional soldier who had enlisted in 1937. He was married, a Roman Catholic in faith, and was from Kreuznach. Said to be a quiet man and non-political.

The discussion groups continued weekly and a radio, used mainly for news from London or Hamburg, was listened to when conditions allowed. At the Ross Hostel, under Camp Leader S/Fw Wilhelm Guenther 'B-', there was some effort to get the POWs into contact with Ross people to counter strong anti-German feelings. To this end a Free Church club was set up on a Saturday afternoon. Despite this, Ross council, unlike Gloucester or Cheltenham, refused to allow Germans to attend council meetings due to these anti-German feelings. The entire hostel population of 200 Germans attended the various churches in Ross to celebrate Christmas Mass with the locals.

Whilst no reference is made in the files studied, it appears that following the Italian departure from Newent Hostel it was re-occupied by German POWs. A local newspaper report of Tuesday, 24 December read:

> POWS IN 'THE MESSIAH' AT NEWENT. A number of German prisoners of war, one of whom sang the tenor solos, were amongst the local choir and orchestra that gave a performance of 'The Messiah' in St Mary's church, Newent. Under the conductorship of the rector (Rev. C.J.K. Burnell) the choir and orchestra acquitted themselves with distinction …

Highnam Court Hostel SO 794 194, 14 May 1948.[13]

On Boxing Day, 26 December the paper reported:

> The Celebrations at Newent 1946. Christmastide in Newent was spent very quietly.
> On Christmas Eve and Christmas morning the town band played selections and carols
> in the streets. All the services at the churches in the town had been well attended.
> At the parish church many communicants attended the various services. The Rector
> (Rev. C.J.K. Burnell) officiated. German prisoners of war at the local camp were
> invited out to tea on Christmas Day to the various places where they are employed.[14]

The Germans continued their political rehabilitation and re-education by visiting
Gloucester council meetings as well as Gloucester Cathedral and the city museums.

 THE NATIONAL POSITION

Repatriations resulted in a number of POW transfers to transit camps, with many
camps closing or being administered by just one camp. In the case of Gloucestershire,
the administration was taken over by Camp 263 Leckhampton Court around late
October/November 1947.

The national figures for German POWs was 380,000 in September 1946 with
3,000 a month being sent home. The government under Prime Minister Attlee was

Churcham Hostel
SO 766 189,
9 April 1947.[15]

most reluctant to repatriate these POWs as much work was still required in Britain. With the winter of 1946 approaching the repatriation rose to 15,000 a month.

The final report of the COGA was for 16 October 1947.[16] The total number of POWs was now given as well over 1,000 in the main camp and its hostels. Llanclowdy was now abandoned but thirty-five POWs were sent with some haste to a camp at Churcham in order, the report states, 'to prevent squatters from taking over the camp'.

Squatters were becoming a problem: they were people made homeless during the war or returning from the armed services. They sought work and accommodation, so often took up residence in now disused military buildings.

One example of this problem is reported in the *Citizen* newspaper dated 18 December 1946:

> … because squatters were now living at both the ex-American NAAS camp near the port of Lydney and at Sudbury they were now to pay rent of six shillings and sixpence and seven shillings and sixpence depending on the condition of the camp huts.

The American barracks were described as substantial and the old POW sector as dilapidated.

4

Joachim Schulze

*An account of his time as a POW in Newtown Hostel
Near Ashchurch, Tewkesbury, 1946–48*

Joachim Schulze returned to Tewkesbury several times in recent years. His POW recollections were published in the *Tewkesbury Historical Society's Bulletin* (No. 21) in 2012 and more details of his wartime experiences were received in correspondence with him. Sadly, Joachim died on 13 January 2013, aged 85.

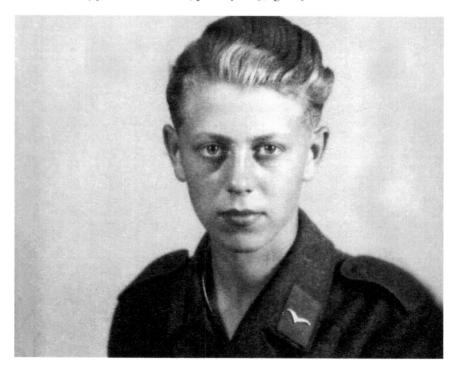

Private Joachim Schulze in his German uniform, aged 17. (Author's collection)

Joachim Schulze was conscripted into the German Army straight from school, aged just 17 years in 1944. He was later captured by the Americans during the Battle of the Bulge (December 1944–January 1945). As he said in our correspondence:

> I was captured on 27 December 1944 at the Luxembourgian village named Syr, very close to the Belgian border. In the chaos there it was quite easy to leave my unit and disappear in a house and wait for the Americans. On the way I was wounded in my left thigh. Was it a German bullet or an American? I don't know. There was another German with me. We were taken to an Army doctor on top of a jeep.[1]

Following hospital treatment he was put on a ship to New York as a POW on 21 March 1945. After a three-day train trip he found himself at Camp Maxey, Texas, on 13 May. There he worked on farms in Texas and later Colorado until the German defeat. Following another long train journey through the Rocky Mountains he was to embark on ship from Long Beach for repatriation to Germany. However, the ship sailed to Liverpool in England where he disembarked on 16 February 1946 and was taken to Moreton-in-Marsh that same day. He confirmed my understanding that the POWs were led to believe they were going home to Germany:

> We were told by the Americans that we were being repatriated. I remember: among the accompanying American officers on board happened to be a captain who was for a short time the commander of my working camp in Colorado! When I met him I said full of joy: 'I'm looking forward to going home?' 'Yes, you are going home.' That was his answer.[2]
>
> I can't remember any assessment and classification on our arrival in Liverpool. When we left the ship we were counted by a GI and at the end of the gangway there was another GI and a Tommy reading our names aloud. Then we were taken right to the waiting train. That's all I can remember.

In relation to the ICRC reports that many German POWs had items of their property stolen by their American military guards, Joachim states: 'We were very often searched by GIs, and I can remember that many a prisoner complained afterwards that some of his belongings were missing.'

Joachim did not spend very long at Moreton-in-Marsh Hostel before a further transfer.

> It was a cold day, that 27 February 1946, when about forty German prisoners of war, carrying their light luggage and accompanied by two British soldiers, marched from the railway station of Ashchurch to 'Camp Newtown' at Tewkesbury.

Camp Newtown was in fact a 'hostel' for working POWs administered at this time by Camp 37, Sudeley Castle, Winchcombe. Joachim describes a camp of four buildings, two for living and sleeping, one for the latrines, washroom and stores, with one room for use by the camp medic and the barber. Finally, one hut was for the canteen and kitchen, with a separate room within for the guards. The camp had two protected personnel: the camp leader who was also the 'Lagersprecher' (spokesman of the camp) and the camp cook.

This type of establishment was fairly typical of the small accommodation units set up by the Ministry of Agriculture to house local workers; there was a similar hostel at Newent. The camp was on the Ashchurch Road, A438. On its eastern side was the first house in Newtown and on the other two sides there were fields with cattle.

Newtown Hostel near Ashchurch, 16 January 1947.[3]

The camp was closed in by barbed wire. Today the Canterbury Leys public house with its beer garden occupies the hostel site.

The Germans arrived at the camp just a few days after the previous occupants, Italian POWs, had left for their repatriation. Joachim recalls:

> They [the Italians] had left behind two black cats, a tom-cat, which mostly was 'on the road', and a queen, which never left the camp, loved to be cuddled and gave birth to four sweet kittens twice a year. Always in anyone's bed! We named the two cats 'Peter' (German pronunciation) and 'Alte' (female form of 'The Old One'). By the way, we always got rid of the kittens on farms where we had already asked permission. Before that, they were everybody's pets and we all used to have a lot of fun with them.

He describes the huts as having the usual bunk beds, some stools and an iron stove that they had to keep running on cold days. We have seen how efficient the Italians were at improvising furniture, but it seems that there were neither cupboards nor tables left for the new occupants and so they found themselves having to look for boxes or other items that they could use to store their possessions. The POWs were provided with the usual palliasses made of stuffed straw, and blankets and other items as supplied at the main camp at Winchcombe. Joachim also remembers the radio reports:

> There was a loudspeaker in the huts that we slept in and, late in the evening, our radio, operated by the English guards, was able to receive a German station. By listening to the reports, we learned a lot about what was happening in post-war Germany. All was quiet when the reports about the War Crime Trials in Nuremberg were transmitted.

The two British guards were a sergeant and a private. Joachim recalls that the sergeant used to call him 'Lofty'. He adds that, as far as he could remember, the guards were all friendly, helpful 'comrades' and did not bother the POWs.

Every night after ten, one of them went through the huts and counted the prisoners. On some occasions, however, the guards with additional support carried out unannounced searches at night. They searched the rooms, beds, clothes and the prisoners' belongings as well as full-body searches. They were looking for things that the prisoners were not allowed to possess, for example, money. (Prisoners were awarded

German prisoners later dyed their uniforms black or dark blue (although printed here in black and white). (Author's collection)

tokens to use as money in their canteen.) On one occasion, he remembers that the
soldiers did find some money. Apparently some farmers were paying the prisoners for
overtime in cash. Whilst this was initially illegal, as time progressed and repatriation was
under way, prisoners were then allowed to receive money from the farmers. By this
time, searches were no longer deemed necessary and were stopped.

The previous camp reports from the ICRC had all recorded that the food was good
in both quality and quantity but here we see that this view is not shared. Joachim
claims that neither was the case and in terms of quality it was definitely too little for a
growing young man. In many cases the farmers, when made aware of the food deficit,
gave out extra rations to the prisoners working with them. Farmers who did not
offer additional rations were made known to other prisoners, who would try to avoid
going to these farms. The camp did receive some supplies delivered by the NAAFI,
and the POWs could purchase other items of food as well as additional cigarettes.

The situation, as far as the German POWs were concerned, was rapidly changing
once the war had ended. The War Cabinet met on Friday, 18 May 1945 chaired by the
prime minister himself, the Right Hon. Winston Churchill. They examined just what
tasks the prisoners could undertake in rebuilding the country and its infrastructure.
It was decided that German POWs would now be allowed to be billeted on farms
and other work locations where hostel accommodation was not appropriate. It was
also agreed that the type of work undertaken could be extended, no longer limited
to tasks for the Ministry of Agriculture & Fisheries but also to include the following
areas of employment:[4]

1 Highways
2 Preparation of Housing Sites
3 Railways, Harbours and Docks
4 Public Utilities: Electricity, Gas, Water, Sewage and Hydroelectric
5 Land reclamation and drainage
6 Coastal erosion and defences
7 Building Materials

Joachim Schulze undertook a number of jobs whilst held at Newtown Hostel in 1946
as these changes took place. He recalls:

> We worked on farms or we dug ditches for irrigation and laid the pipes. On farms
> we had to do all kinds of work. We got to the workplaces on foot, by bike, by bus or
> by lorries. We worked in groups or single.
>
> In winter, when working on farms was limited, we were used for shovelling snow
> in town. Many a resident gave us a 'cuppa'. As we did not want to behave impolitely,
> we drank every cup being offered. In the evening, we were filled up with tea and
> had a troubled night!

Sometimes we worked with 'land-girls', as they were called. They wore a uniform with a badge on one sleeve with the letters WLA (Women's Land Army). When we asked what those letters meant, they used to answer: 'Winston's Little Angels'! As they were of our age or younger, we were very interested in them, and quite a few became a 'little angel' for some of us.

The farmers, and their workers we were with, were friendly and treated us like normal people and not as adversaries. That's why I have only good memories of England and the English.

It was not always plain sailing and one incident nearly killed him:

I remember a day when I was on a one-horse cart and the horse's bit loosened. As I pulled the reins, the whole bridle slipped off and down to the bottom of the neck. The horse was not under my control any more. It began to canter and soon to gallop from the field right into the road and bolted as fast as it could. It was a downhill road, too. I sat on the cart pulling the reins, pressing my feet against the front board, crying and frightened to death. We endangered cars and motorbikes, cyclists and pedestrians. The horse kept racing back through many curves and bends. Then it slowed down, went into its farmyard and stopped right in front of its stable – I HAD SURVIVED!

Re-education was an important aspect of British policy with the COGA running lectures, visits and film shows to introduce the German prisoners to the concept of democracy prior to their repatriation. The Sudeley Camp had an active programme of re-education as previously shown and these activities, we were told, extended to the main camp hostels, which included Newtown, but Joachim claims that these measures were not established at his hostel. He was aware of the relaxation in security which he describes as a step-by-step approach to his re-education activities. What follows was, in fact, the government's re-education policy.

The first step was writing letters and receiving them. Then they tore down the barbed wire and replaced it by a simple fence. After that, we were allowed to go to services. The Catholic church was the first. We all went there: both Catholics and Protestants. After that we asked the Protestant church for the parson to come into our camp and conduct a service in German. We asked him to open up his church for us to attend the regular service. He did, and so we were able to go to services in the famous Tewkesbury Abbey.

Another step was the permission to go out for walks on Sundays and after work, too. At 10 p.m. we had to be back. Then followed shopping, paying visits, being 'billeted' (that meant living on the farm), attending theatres, cinemas etc. (but never pubs!), going by bus and train, fraternisation, marrying an English girl, getting 'dismissed' in order to work and live on farms, thus becoming a civilian.

Not to be forgotten are the lots of parcels we sent home with things that were rare in stricken Germany. Last, but not least, during all this period, German immigrants came into the camps, gave lectures – mostly political topics – and discussions with us. At this time, cinema shows were introduced when a German prisoner was sent from camp to camp with a portable screen, film projector and the necessary equipment. This was all arranged after work in the evening in the canteen. We saw mostly non-political German films, and English or American films with subtitles.

This is most interesting, especially when Joachim talks of German immigrants coming and giving talks. The documents on record list all speakers and they all had to be registered. They then had to take a short course in the correct procedures to follow within their talks. Whilst several nationalities are given, including British speakers, none are listed as of German nationality. The films were on loan from the YMCA or sometimes the local WEA.

Like his fellow POWs, Joachim was allowed to leave the camp at Christmas 1947 to be taken in by an English family. He went to have Christmas with a local family who had befriended him. He told me that he had made a number of English friends during these latter days who made him feel at home and of whom he retained fond memories.

Joachim remembers the start of the repatriations in the summer of 1947. The hostels began to close and the prisoners were transferred back to the main camp at Sudeley, near Winchcombe.

In the case of Newtown, evacuation occurred quickly as the area around Tewkesbury had one of its notorious floods, with the floodwater reaching the hostel on 20 March 1947. The prisoners from Newtown Hostel continued to provide labour in and around Tewkesbury and were brought from Sudeley Camp by local buses or lorries.

The POWs certainly had a lot more freedom in these latter days as they waited their turn to return home, and many prisoners had access to bicycles.

Joachim recalls cycling to his friend's home in Tewkesbury on a Sunday for a meal, or going into Cheltenham by bus or hitchhiking, often with his fellow POWs. He says that they stopped for a sixpenny bag of fish and chips and that there was always a long queue of prisoners there with many more crowded around the front of the shop.

I suppose the owner became a rich man through us! After that I usually went to the pictures. And sometimes an English person paid the admission. There was only one cinema that did not permit German prisoners.

In Winchcombe camp, there was a football field and we had a team that played other camps. The players were equipped by the Army and taken around by lorries, sometimes with spectators. There was also a German POW band, equipped by the British Army and called the 'HMK Band', after the conductor Heinz-Meyer-Kundt who, by day, was the dentist's assistant. They had no singer and played old German songs and hits: one day the band gave a concert for the residents of Winchcombe and the German POWs.

With more and more POWs returning to Germany the camp became almost empty and eventually closed down on 20 January 1948. Joachim and his comrades were transferred to Camp 263 Leckhampton, near Cheltenham, before again moving to camps in Bristol. Eventually, on 7 May, he was moved to a camp in Bury St Edmunds before embarking at Harwich for Germany on 13 May 1948.

One can only imagine the many thoughts and emotions felt at this time by the returning POWs. Joachim Schulze had been away from his family for almost four years and really did not know just what awaited his return.

Joachim's postscript:

After I returned home, I went to a teachers training college, and I was a teacher in East Germany until 1955. I left there because I was fed up with another dictatorship. Since my stay in England I wanted to live in a democracy. In West Germany I started with a study again to achieve a higher grade. My wife was also a teacher; I retired in 1989. We have two sons: one is a vocational school teacher here in Braunschweig and the other is a surgeon in Berlin. I have four grandchildren – two sets of twins!

5

Camps 649, 554 & 555

Company (Coy) Working Camps for Italian Co-operators:
Swindon Village Camp 649, Woodfield Farm Churchdown Camp 554
and Newark House Hempstead Camp 555

Italy surrendered to the Allied Forces on 8 September 1943, but this surrender was to pose serious legal and logistical problems for the British Government. Whilst the Italians had lain down their arms, severe fighting continued between the Allies and the German Army that still occupied much of Northern Italy.

The British War Cabinet had approved the use of Italian POWs for essential labour, under the Geneva Convention, and since February 1941 they had been used to supplement the labour force. By 1943 there were estimated to be more than 75,000 Italian prisoners working in Britain; they were seen as a docile labour force, not as a burden but as a major contribution to the war effort.[1]

The Americans were soon to realise that they too were using Italian prisoners for the war effort but with a pending presidential election were very aware that there were about 600,000 American-Italian voters to be considered.

Eventually the Italians became co-belligerents or 'wartime partners'. In other words the Italians switched sides to cooperate with the Allied Forces against Germany and her Axis partners, but without any formal treaty of military alliance with the Allied nations. This agreement was to last from 1943 until the German surrender in 1945.[2]

America and Britain were in disagreement as to how to treat the Italian prisoners and many lengthy discussions took place through the spring and summer of 1943. The Americans had allowed recently captured Italian troops in Sicily to be paroled to their homes in order to work their farms, thereby relieving them of having to house and feed a substantial number of Italian prisoners. Shortly afterwards these prisoners, classified as being on parole, were released without consultation with the British Allies.

… the British and the Americans had control of more than 500,000 Italian prisoners, and decisions had to be made about their future. As Italy was effectively changing sides in the middle of the war, for which the Geneva Convention of 1929 made no provision, there were conflicting views on how the prisoners should now be treated.

Italy had captured 75,000 British servicemen in North Africa and the Mediterranean, and it was hoped that they would be made available as part of a prisoner exchange after the Italian surrender. The Germans, however, were well aware of the situation and quickly removed many of the British POWs to camps in Belgium and Germany. With the loss of these British prisoners all agreements with the new Italian Government were cancelled. The Italian authorities were now informed that Italian POWs held in Britain would only be repatriated immediately after the last German had been expelled from Italy.

> As the Italian prisoner-of-war camps in Britain were reported to be full of 'effervescence' upon learning of the surrender, and prisoners were beginning to ask questions, the government feared that they might become discontented and unwilling to work.[3]

Negotiations with the new Badoglio government dragged on until April 1944 with no apparent agreement as to the fate of the Italian POWs held in British and American hands. A decision was made that further negotiation was pointless and in fact could affect Badoglio's political position. As a result the Allies decided to continue to rely on Badoglio's verbal agreement made with Eisenhower in October 1943, which assumed that Italian prisoners could be used in any and all non-combatant employment.

The Italian POWs were reclassified as voluntary co-operators: they could help the war effort or, if declining this offer, they would remain in POW camps until the war was over. In agreeing to become a co-operator these Italians were to undertake a variety of work, including war work, and in exchange they would have fewer restrictions, greater freedom, and national pay and conditions of employment. Many of these new 'co-operators' were not prepared to undertake work that they felt was in breach of their rights under the Geneva Convention.

The position is well summed up in a paper by Kent Fedorowich and Bob Moore when they conclude:

> Attempts to find a more flexible way of using Italians after the surrender foundered on the legal problems of their status, the need for control and the Badoglio government's refusal to agree that they should remain prisoners of war. Ultimately, the Allies wanted it both ways. They needed a labour force and they wanted it to perform any task associated with the war effort. To control it, however, they had to treat it as prisoners, which prohibited them from asking it to do much of the work they wanted done.[4]

To get around the constraints of the Geneva Convention, the Allies fell back on the verbal agreement of October 1943 that 'Italians might be used for all types of work in the Allied cause'.

The result was that those POWs captured early in the war remained as POWs in Britain, whilst those captured later were paroled, sent home and some even fought against the Germans to help liberate their country. Needless to say, some of the POWs held in Britain after the Italian surrender, and Italy's change of status to co-belligerent, were greatly disappointed at remaining prisoners of war.

The following document is a War Cabinet Memorandum dated 14 September 1943, written by Sir Percy James Grigg, then Secretary of State for War:[5]

Position of Italian Prisoners of War After Armistice
Memorandum by the Secretary of State for War

1   At the meeting of the War Cabinet on 13 September 1943 I mentioned that, as a result of the Armistice with Italy, Italian prisoners of war in this country were asking camp commandants about their future, and I suggested that, unless a suitable answer was given, there was a risk that they might become discontented and that their work would be affected. The War Cabinet agreed that this matter should be considered later in the week, in conjunction with a Memorandum circulated by the Lord President of the Council.

2   I understand that it has since been suggested that it would be helpful to the War Cabinet if I were to circulate the text of an aide memoire for the guidance of commandants in charge of Italian prisoners of war camps in this country, which has been drawn up at official level in the Foreign Office and the War Office, and which I read to the War Cabinet at yesterday's meeting. The proposed text is reproduced below:

'The cessation of hostilities with Italy as a result of the signing of the Armistice does not of itself make any difference under International Law to the status of Italians held in this country. They remain prisoners of war. We shall continue to treat them with respect and all consideration. Discipline must however be maintained and orders obeyed. All Italians must realise that their country is short of food and other necessities, in obtaining which she must look to the United Nations for assistance. They are urged to work hard in this country because by so doing they will be helping their families in Italy.'

P. J. Grigg

The War Office, S. W. 1
14th September 1943.

━━◀━ SWINDON VILLAGE ITALIAN COY CAMP 649 ━━◀━

Swindon Hall and Swindon Manor, along with other large buildings, were requisitioned by the War Office in 1939 and Nissen huts were then built on much of the land surrounding Swindon Hall. These huts were for other ranks and the officers were billeted in the larger buildings. The hall was surrounded by a number of trees that included cedars, Wellingtonias, Douglas firs, beech, acacia and a lime tree in front of the hall.

The photograph of the camp shows these huts along the main driveway to the hall, on land that is now used as playing fields: they were intended to be used as a transit camp for British soldiers.

Following the retreat of the British and Allied Forces from the Battle of Dunkirk (26 May–4 June 1940), these huts and the hall were used to house a number of units, including the Royal Engineers (who arrived with a large collection of pontoon bridge sections), the South Lancashire Regiment and the Welsh Fusiliers. A number of names can still be seen written on some of the wooden beams in the attic of Swindon Hall. Some of these are recorded as Pt M.H. Boddison (20 February 1941), C.W. Bissiker 9658117, Sapper Scanlon, and Lance Corporal Hubbard.[6]

Swindon Village near Cheltenham, showing the Italian POW camp behind Swindon Hall, SO 936 249, 1 April 1946.[7]

Swindon Hall. (Author's collection)[8]

There was a report of a fire some time during the winter of 1941/2 that caused considerable damage to the roof and west corner of the hall. Despite the damage it was not until 28 August 1942 that Captain G.B. Frasun of the War Department, Land Branch (Southern Command), gave notice of their surrender of the hall. (Damage had rendered it uninhabitable until after the war. It was restored in 1949 and converted into five separate flats.)

Eventually Bruton Knowles Estate Agents, acting for their clients, sent a letter on 4 February 1943 stating that their clients (given as John Bubb) had agreed to compensation at £85 per annum from 28 August 1942 to 3 February 1943. This claim included removing cables and electric wires, and repairing damage done to the floor. The military maintained occupation of the land around the hall and manor house, including what would become the Italian POW Working Camp.[9]

The following notes are extracts from the British Pioneer Corps war diaries with some explanations inserted by the author.[10]

The new working companies were planned under the same format used by the British Pioneer Corps. The Italians were formed into 8–10 sections comprising twenty-eight men in each section, so that a company (Coy) would total between 233 and 280 men. Each section was put under the command of an Italian sergeant. The British command for the Pioneer Corps consisted of a major in command, then a captain as a second in command, followed by two lieutenants.

The camp behind Swindon Village Hall would be home to a number of Italian Coy working companies, the first of which was 554 Coy and then 649 Coy.

ITALIAN WORKING CAMP 554 COY

This company was formed on 1 January 1944 in Buxton, Derbyshire, under Major N. de P. MacRoberts (10862) as officer in command. Major MacRoberts was to remain the OC of 554 Coy until it was disbanded in December 1945. The company arrived at Swindon Village, Cheltenham, on 8 January 1944.[11]

Ninety-seven Italian volunteers were taken on the company's strength from POW Camp 114 Eden Vale, Wiltshire; they were put to work immediately on road construction and salvage work.

Officers joining 554 Coy in March and April were Captain A.G. Belfrage MC (119772) as second in command, Lt W. Brown (250912), Lt R.A. Woods MM (139339), and Lt H.G. Bloodworth (112264) from 563 Coy.

The camp was visited by Dr J. Wirth of the ICRC on 28 April 1944 when the camp capacity was said to be 350 POWs; on the date of the visit there were a total of 223 Italians (10 sections). He describes this new type of co-operator camp in his report as follows:[12]

> The entire camp is organised in sections of 20 to 26 men and commanded by a British Sergeant and also having an Italian NCO Leader (Sergeant Major Giuseppe Giovino).
>
> The camp has no compound, no barb wire and all the prisoners (the Italians in these camps are deemed to be prisoners) are allowed to move around but with certain restrictions within quite a large area around the camp. Up to 10 to 12 kilometres of roads are available to them. On the other hand the restrictions are as follows:- The prisoners must keep absolutely to the paths and roads. They are not allowed in certain areas within that large perimeter and above all they are subject to censorship and must in no circumstances mix with the population. In fact they all had to sign a declaration to agree this but when a number of them refused to do that the authorities accepted a formal notice rather than individual signatures. It is interesting to note here that these prisoners were not selected at all but on the contrary they were sent to these camps on some sort of experimental basis absolutely randomly.
>
> The British personnel is reduced to an absolute minimum, there is no armed guard. Policing of the camp is done by the Italian prisoners themselves and a number of them wear arm bands.[13]

Each of the Nissen huts housed 12 prisoners, so each section had two huts allocated to them. Heating was provided by two coal stoves and each prisoner was provided with a camp bed and five blankets. The kitchens, toilets, washrooms and shower blocks were built in brick.

The Italian co-operators were entitled to food rations drawn up in June 1942 but were allowed a small increase as a reward for their compliance. There was an increase in the cheese ration 6 days out of 7 rather than 4 days, 24oz of potatoes rather than 16oz, dried vegetables 1oz 3 times a week rather than 1oz once a week, and the ration also included 2½ pence per person per day in cash. This money was for purchasing tinned meat, pasta, spices and sauces. The prisoners who worked outside the camp and took a cold meal for lunch received an extra allocation of money; this could go up to a shilling a day, and could only be used to purchase food products that were available in quantity on the open market. These restrictions were War Office based but generally the prisoners were not happy with them and they often caused complaints.

> The Italian kitchen is well constructed and extremely well run by Italian cooks who have control over the quantity of rations which are distributed. It has to be repeated that even taking into account additions the base ration is still higher in calories than those of British troops.
>
> The work carried out at the camp is strictly limited according to the Convention. POWs work in teams on mending roads and in the stores for non-military materials. The work is carried out satisfactorily. About 7% of the total number of POWs makes up the camp personnel as elsewhere. The difference here is that this group of personnel includes a certain number of men who are working as military police. The Commandant said that the POWs do all these activities willingly with a clear preference for building works where they can see the results of their labour.
>
> The POWs complain vigorously, for in their minds the work they are asked to do seems to be of a military nature. The Camp Commandant assures us that the authorities are taking every precaution, so that the occupations carried out by the POWs remain strictly within the limits of what is allowed by the Convention.[14]

The work asked of the men was sometimes seen by them to be a breach of the Geneva Convention and it led to prisoners refusing to work on occasion. More on this issue will be revealed when accounts of 555 Coy are given, but it is of interest that these Italians, whose government was now said to be supporting the Allied cause, were still reluctant to undertake work that they saw as helping Britain to win the war against the Germans.

> The pay awarded to the prisoners is effectively the same as those received in agricultural camps at this time. As a general rule, pay was 1½ pence an hour and a shilling a day. In fact this sum is paid to all POWs no matter how long their journey takes them. Or time lost due to bad weather. The only complaint and cause of dissatisfaction with the POWs, and where they are unwilling to work, is when their pay is reduced to just three farthings an hour [three quarters of a penny]. Likewise the military pay for soldiers is one shilling eleven and a half pence a week and sergeants two shillings nine and a half pence a week. Camp personnel are paid by the welfare fund at 1½ penny an hour for a day of 8 hours. The accounting system is the same as elsewhere. The POWs are paid in camp money and must use it in the camp canteen. There was no complaint about this.[15]

The prisoners were provided with a number of leisure activities. The ICRC report highlights that a large number of games and sports were played by the men. The library, however, was poor and the camp had no gramophone. On the other hand the prisoners had a radio and they could listen to all stations, both British and Continental.

As far as walks were concerned, they could go out without escort within a limited area around the camp but they had to keep to the roads. A Catholic priest from the neighbourhood, who spoke Italian, regularly said Mass and the average attendance was about sixty. Twenty illiterate personnel attended evening classes organised by the local YMCA. This organisation regularly showed two films a week which the men appreciated.

The POWs asked the inspector if he could advise them on what their actual situation was and what was to come for their future. 'In spite of what we ourselves know we were unable to respond, even partially, to this worry which is totally understandable.'

The Italian POWs were gradually reduced in number as their work was required in other areas of the county. By late July detachments were sent from Swindon Village to work in Gloucester, Ashchurch and Lydney.

A further forty-five Italians arrived on 13 August and, on the orders of 52 Group Command, the OC read out the instructions concerning the difference between co-operators and non-co-operators.[16]

Two Italian bakers and two butchers were sent to undertake trade tests at Tidworth in Wiltshire on 26 August 1944.

The POWs from 554 Coy were now disbursed from Swindon with 104 being transferred to 555 Coy at Churchdown on 17 September, and a further seventy-nine moved to Newark House, Monks Meadow, Hempstead, Gloucester, on 24 September.

This movement between working companies was very common as the Italians were needed in a number of locations where work was required. As well as Italians who had previously been in POW Camps throughout Britain, more Italian POW 'volunteers' were arriving from North Africa, America and other Commonwealth locations.

Those Italians left at Swindon were working at Gloucester Regional Salvage Unit (RSU) on roads and salvage during October, with sixteen then sent to 192 General Hospital in Cirencester for drainage work.

The following work details are listed in the Pioneer Corps war diaries.

24 October 1944:	12 men were sent to chief Royal Engineer in Ashchurch.
10 December 1944:	102 Italian workers under the command of Lt W. Brown were sent to Quedgeley Camp. (This is almost certainly Quedgeley Court Camp 142.)

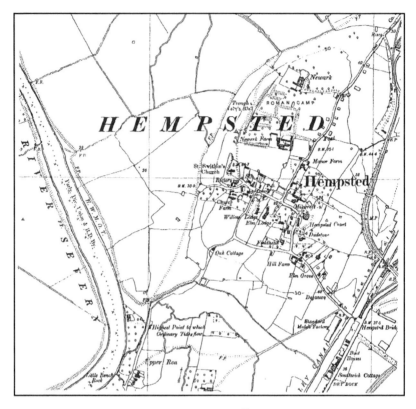

Newark House and Newark Farm, OS map 1938. [17]

1 January 1945:	Italian 554 Coy was relocated at Newark House in Gloucester. The men are now working at the Gas Works and at Llanthony Docks. Swindon Village Camp was occupied on 2 December 1944 by Italian Coy 649.
9 February 1945:	Three sections from 554 were attached to Coy 649 at Swindon Hall, Cheltenham.
17 February:	The whole company is again moved and this time to Woodfield Farm, Brockworth Road, Churchdown. (This camp will be discussed under Coy 555.)
29 April 1945:	100 men are sent to Winchcombe for one day loading trains.
1 July 1945:	43 POWs are transferred to Camp 649.
14 August 1945:	All POWs were confined to Camp for two days. No explanation is given for this.
25 August 1945:	There was a football match with the camp taking on Camp 649 as well as a boxing tournament in the afternoon.
27 September 1945:	There was a YMCA concert for the men.
19 November 1945:	A football match, this time with 578 Coy.

554 Coy were still at Woodfield Farm Camp, Brockworth Road, Churchdown, during December and the last entry, on 31 December 1945, indicated that the Italians were repatriated early in 1946.

ITALIAN WORKING CAMP 649 COY

Camp 649 Italian POW Coy (originally 624 Coy) was formed in North Africa in 1944. Italian POWs were encouraged to volunteer for work in Britain where they were promised better conditions, more freedom, and fair payment for their labour. They were also assured that they would be helping their country, which was now on the side of the Allies.

On 1 December 1944, the newly formed company were at sea. The Coy was commanded by Captain E.J. Gooch (171767) and two Italian Officers, Captain E. Grimaldi (T/36358) and Lt R. Gianneti (T/32105). The company disembarked at Glasgow on 2 December 1944.[18] They arrived in Cheltenham the following day and moved to Swindon Village Camp that afternoon. Lieutenant Welsh (142809) was taken on strength. (Some reports refer to Swindon Manor Camp but these are the same.)

4 December 1944:	The Coy was placed under 77 Group Command who were in overall command of the administration of 649 Coy and other Italian working Coy. (This included both 554 and 555 Italian Working Coy.)
8 December 1944:	The majority of the prisoners were now sent to work under the control of the Deputy Chief of the Royal Engineers (DCRE) and a further group of eighteen men were sent to work with seventy-two mobile Field Bakery. The Italians worked a six-day week with ideally Sundays being a day of rest but other days could be taken if seven or more days support was required.
9 December 1944:	624 Coy was re-designated as 649 Coy.
10 December 1944:	Eight sections (about 244 men) were sent to Nettlebed Camp in Oxfordshire. Nettlebed was used by RAF Woodcote 70 Maintenance Unit (MU) and was also used as a POW camp to house Italian POWs.
13 December 1944:	Captain E.J. Gooch was promoted to the rank of major and as a consequence Captain E.E. Palmer (197692) was taken on as second in command.
23 December 1944:	Lt F.G. Johnson and Second Lt G. Taylor are taken on strength. Lt Johnson's name no longer appears on the War Diary entry for 30 December, but Lt Welsh and the two Italian officers are still listed.

30 January 1945:	649 Coy is still at Swindon Hall. Second Lt G. Taylor is taken off strength and transferred to 389 Coy.[19]
9 February 1945:	610 Coy is now attached to Swindon Village Coy 649 and sixty-nine of these new men were posted to 554 Coy. This movement of Italian POWs between placements was very common as workers were needed for a variety of work. The following entry demonstrates this.
12 February 1945:	17 men at Badgeworth Court 3 men Swindon Hall – Agriculture 18 men to Ashchurch demolition with DCRE 9 men (attached to 554 Coy for salvage Depot Cheltenham) 20 men to Down Ampney laying pipe 43 men Reserve Store Depot (RSD) Gloucester (RSD dealt with damaged uniforms and equipment)
28 March 1945:	160 men at 173 Ordnance Depot at Didcot.

The diary accounts for this period show a number of British Pioneer Corps personnel being moved around the area, as well as many Italian sections being temporarily attached to a number of other Coy units. Major E.J. Gooch was taken off the numbers and sent as officer commanding 661 POW Coy at Eynsham Hall in Witney.

10 September 1945:	The following detachments of men are recorded and demonstrate the wide range of occupation undertaken by the Italians:

17 — in agriculture
 7 — Swindon Village
21 — DCRE North Gloucestershire
 7 — Cheltenham DCRE
10 — DCRE Cirencester
20 — DCRE Daglingworth
 7 — salvage work at Cheltenham
 8 — to Reservoir Camp
19 — to officer in command Barracks in Cirencester
 8 — Moreton-in-Marsh
31 — to Andoversford attached to 554 Coy
 6 — to Bristol
30 — DCRE Horfield Barracks
 2 — Bristol Garrison

The last diary entry is dated 31 December 1945 and simply lists three officers: Major R.E. Watts, Captain W.N. Weedon and Lt A.E. Symon. It would appear that the Italians from 649 Coy were repatriated about this time. There is no record of any German POWs being placed at Swindon Hall.

Although the Italians were at Swindon Hall for a very short time, they are still remembered by the villagers. These are just a few comments recorded by them in the Swindon Village Local History Project.[20]

> The POWs were friendly chaps. They made jewellery from scraps of Perspex, small pieces of aluminium alloy and coloured toothbrush handles. Rings were made from aluminium melted in a spoon and cast into grooves in a brick which had been made with a nail.
> The officers were quite colourful and they wore light blue uniforms.
> The Italians put on a wonderful exhibition of their work. There were all sorts of crafts including woodworking.
> In Brockhampton lane there was a small 'Osier' bed and the Italians used these willows to make baskets.
> Italians tried to teach me Italian and I tried to teach them English.
> They were allowed out of camp on parole but had large coloured cloth diamonds sewn on their uniforms.
> They were employed on local farms and they fitted well in the community.

ITALIAN WORKING CAMP, 555 COY

This Italian working company was formed in Buxton, Derbyshire, at the Empire Hotel on 28 December 1943, and sent three days later – 31 December 1943 – to the POW cage at the County Ground, Swindon in Wiltshire, to collect seventy-eight Italian POWs. The officer in command was Major C.J. McNamara (49241), also Captain H.S. Armstrong (68711) as second in command with lieutenants W.N. Weedon (142808) and J.T. Harrison (171064).[21]

The company moved to Stratton Factory Camp, Swindon, on 15 February 1944 and, taking on further groups of Italian co-operators, reached company strength of 247 men (about ten sections).

On 28 February, thirty-three men refused to work. A week later this number had increased to 168 men refusing to work at what they considered to be work of a military nature. Authorisation was given to the CO to convert the camp into a detention barracks and co-operator status was withdrawn.

When confirmation was received over the POWs' status as non-co-operators, the 168 men were removed to a detention camp. The remaining sections were moved to Woodfield Farm Camp, Brockworth Road, Churchdown, on 25 March 1944.

The unrest continued despite the move to Woodfield Farm, with a further 153 POWs confined to the camp for refusing to work. On 13 April another twenty-seven POWs were sent to Camp 12 in Edinburgh.[22]

Some men are reported to be working on 14 April:

50 — road construction Charlton Kings US Camp
40 — road construction Toddington
45 — agricultural work at Blockley
20 — at unserviceable Clothing Depot Gloucester
 8 — barrack Stores ESA
39 — camp duties

Whilst the POW unrest continued into May, Dr J. Wirth of the ICRC paid a visit to the camp on the afternoon of the same day that he inspected Camp 554 as reported above.[24]

The Italian camp leader was Sergeant Major Moscatelli, the camp capacity was 300, and the actual number on the day of the visit was 216 in the main camp with two in a military hospital.

> ... The camp's official title is Working Company 555 [but] the authorities still wish
> it to be known as POW Camp 555. The Prisoners of these camps are in effect still
> considered as prisoners and have not been selected in any way. The authorities asked
> them to make an agreement not to take advantage of the liberties that were being

Woodfield Farm Camp
OS 889 190, 1 April 1946.[23]

given to them and not to fraternise with the civilian population, however those who refused to sign this promise receive the same conditions as their colleagues. In our opinion these working companies are an initial experiment whose aim is to determine what will be the reaction of the entire cohort of the Italian Prisoners without taking into account their previous attitude and organised under the English Pioneer Company model.[25]

The camp is situated in a large country estate. The dormitories are Nissen huts and the whole layout of the camp is no different from that described for agricultural camps and other working companies that we have visited. A basic difference does exist however: there are no enclosures wires or otherwise to separate this camp from the surrounding countryside. At some time the British military guard has been succeeded by an Italian Police Force. As far as the accommodation goes the camp leader has absolutely no complaints to make.

Sergeant Major Moscatelli approached the ICRC inspector regarding a small grievance that the CO had investigated and could not change. The camp leader then threatened to resign if he couldn't get satisfaction. 'All our discussions came to nothing and we have a very clear impression that it's a case not only of narrow mindedness but actually it's a deliberate belligerent act on the part of the Camp Leader.' Dr Wirth concluded that there were certain difficult elements within the group who were putting pressure on the camp leader to cause problems.

Another incident, the men having come back from work at 5.30 and a lorry arriving at the stores that same moment, an English sergeant asked the Camp Leader to identify 5 men to help unload the provision, the Camp Leader refused to look for 5 men and no volunteers stepped forward.[26]

The report highlights that the relations were still tense between the authorities and the prisoners. The POWs were not yet comfortable with the new relations that the British authorities were trying to develop between the Italians and the English.

The other two camps which are similar that we visited are longer established and perhaps for that reason the co-operation there was excellent. The Camp Leader admitted that the supplied food was absolutely sufficient.

Dr Wirth makes a note in his report that: 'As in the other working companies these categories (of work) are excavation and stores work on para military material. The prisoners show a noticeable preference for the excavation work.'

The report does give a list of provisions supplied to the camp for one week. It must be remembered that foodstuffs were in short supply to the local population in 1944 and some locals were resentful that the POWs were given more than them.

30lb	tinned spam	40lb pork sausage
72lb	meat roll	30lb of brawn
48tins 1kg each, baked beans		218 pork pies
7lb	custard powder	225lb of macaroni
109	Swiss rolls	

The POWs had the same leisure facilities as reported above but were reminded that when out walking they must not mix with the civilian population in general or make acquaintance with young girls in particular.

The discontent appears to have continued as 114 men were recorded as 'Non-Co-operators in camp'. A week later the following work details are recorded: [27]

11 *May* 1944

29 – working on roads at Cheltenham Racecourse

39 – working on roads at Toddington

8 – working at DCRE Ashchurch and Andoversford

12 – working on coal at Moreton-in-Marsh

43 – working at unserviceable clothing:

   20 Andoversford, 11 Whittington, 12 Springhill

17 – men at RCD Gloucester

63 – men on Camp duties. [28]

Lieutenant L. Romeo (379383), an Italian officer, was taken on strength on 26 May 1944 and following this appointment there are no entries within the 555 war diaries of any further refusal to work.

On 16 August thirty-one men were available but awaiting passport photographs. Later in September forty-three men were in camp awaiting inoculation.

Apart from Lt. L. Romeo, two other Italian officers were taken on strength: Lt. F. Patroncini (510054) and Medical Officer Second Lt. R. Bolognesi (495649). On 2 December, Cheltenham and Gloucester were placed out of bounds to all Italian POWs. No reason is recorded.

Major C.J. McNamara (49241) the OC is listed for the diary entry for 20 December 1944 but a new OC is given on 30 January 1945: Major T.J.A. Rogers (27966).

On 13 February 1945, 555 Coy is moved to Haig Lines, Crookham, Aldershot, joining 30 Group command. A few days later 554 Coy moved into Woodfield Farm. 555 Coy moved to a number of locations outside the county of Gloucestershire during 1945 until, as in the other war diaries examined, the entries cease on 31 December 1945.

The following report was written by Major Rogers, OC to the Headquarters of Number 106 Group Pioneer Corps, and is given here to show what happened to this group of Italian Co-operators. [29]

This Company was formed as a POW Company at Swindon on 28th December 1943. At first many of the men did not wish to become Co-operators but they were promised certain privileges and so consented. The Company was transferred to Churchdown, Gloucestershire, on 25th March 1944 where the work was confined almost entirely to RCD and RSD Depots at Gloucester. There they had plenty of Huts and were able to have a Canteen, a Macaroni Room, a Church, an Italian Sergeants Mess, Shower Baths, Drying Room, School and Sports Room. At first they were allowed to go to Dances. Many purchased bicycles and were able to take full advantage of the five mile limit.

The work was not arduous and the transport arrangements such that sometimes men did not leave for work before 09.00 hours and were always back in Camp by 17.00 hours. If a shuttle service had to be run some left work at 15.30 hours. A few were on Agricultural work and their hours of labour were as above. They had bedsteads. Just before leaving Churchdown the privilege of using bicycles was withdrawn and the men had to sell them in a prescribed time. The withdrawing of this privilege and also the one allowing them to go to Dance halls upset the Co-operators.

On 13th February 1945 a move was made to Haig Lines, Crookham, where again there was good accommodation although the cleanliness left much to be desired. Bedsteads, Canteen, Drying Room, Sports Room and School were all provided. The men worked extremely hard to get the camp clean, winning enormous praise from those who were actively connected with the Camp. Their hours of labour were increased from 08.00 hours to 17.00 hours exclusive of travelling time. The work was either much harder or much more monotonous. Then an order was issued stating they must not enter Restaurants, including the dining rooms of hotels. It was also stated in answer to my query that they must not use wayside cafes. This has caused the men to be very restive. Orders were received on the 26th March 1945 to move the Company to the Sally Lunn Café, Hindhead, on 27th March 1945. Here the accommodation is insufficient. The men sleep on wood floors no bedsteads being provided, unless there are concrete floors as is the case in Nissen Huts. The men are not allowed to enter canteens (NAAFI, YMCA or any canteen reserved for Allied troops) and the accommodation does not allow for a Canteen of reasonable size, capable of holding 150 men, Drying Room, School, or Church to be established. Macaroni Room has been provided at the expense of sleeping accommodation. During the Easter weekend, owing to the inclement weather the men have had to remain in their sleeping quarters.

All this has had a bad effect on the morale of the men many of whom have not seen their native land for 7 years and who have been prisoners for 4 years. Repeated detachments have been made by them to the effect that the British are not to be trusted and two have expressed a wish to be allowed to return to a Concentration Camp. When one considers that this War would have never taken place had our prestige on the Continents of Europe and Asia not been so low, it is incumbent upon us as a Nation to keep the promises made to these men.

They have complained that the Canadians spit at them and insult them but so far I have been unable to substantiate this.

My chief concern is to get the best possible work out of the men to assist the War Effort but this cannot be done if the men are discontented. I therefore suggest the following:-

1. The ban on the use of wayside cafes is removed.
2. The men are allowed to use bicycles if they wish provided they keep within the prescribed five mile limit.
3. That four Nissen Huts be erected so that one portion of the Sally Lunn Café can be used as a Canteen and the other as a Reading and Writing Room. Bedsteads are to be provided when they are available and more sleeping accommodation will be required. A Drying Room is an urgent necessity as the men have to wash their own clothes. One hut could be used for this.
4. The privileges of all Italian Co-operators should be the same irrespective of location or administrative office.

2 April 45, Commanding 555 Italian, WO/166/17704

In 1945 Clement Attlee became the new Prime Minister heading a Labour administration. Ernest Bevin became the new Foreign Secretary and he was anxious to see the Italian POWs repatriated as soon as possible. He submitted a paper to the Cabinet on 10 September 1945 and agreement was reached on 18 September. With formalities completed and transport problems overcome, the final decision to start the repatriation came on 6 November:

> Since the announcement that this will begin in the not too distant future, morale has risen considerably. The knowledge that about 2,000 are to be sent home undoubtedly has helped to lessen the strong anti-British feelings which have arisen.[30]

Repatriation involved not only Italians held in Britain but also those held in other areas of the Commonwealth. The first prisoners were repatriated in December and all were finally returned by the end of July 1946. A few of these men later returned, married, and settled to a new life in the UK.

6

Camp 157

Bourton-on-the-Hill

Bourton-on-the-Hill POW Camp 157, SP 160 321.[1] United States POW European Theatre of Operations (ETO). Enclosure Number 1.

Camp 157 Bourton-on-the-Hill was located between the junction of the A44 from Moreton-in-Marsh and the A424 from Stow-on-the-Wold. It was originally known as the United States POW European Theatre of Operations (ETO) Enclosure No. 1. The photograph on the previous page clearly shows the separate compounds, which were surrounded by double barbed-wire fences. The smaller camp at the top of the picture was the army camp, with a parade and sports ground between the two camps.

Little recorded evidence is available regarding the early construction and the activities of the camps, but we know that it was built for the United States Army in 1942 to cater for the sudden influx of Italian and German prisoners, mainly from the North African campaigns. John Malin records that 'Mr Fred Sanford started to clear the site but it was finally cleared by Mr Jack DaSilva and his son Harold and their workforce'. A War Office report of December 1942 records that there were 500 POW officers held in the camp.

German prisoners were marched the 4 miles from Moreton-in-Marsh railway station, often during the night and waking the local residents in Bourton with their singing of 'Deutschland, Deutschland über Alles'. Others caused local offence when they urinated at the side of the road or others, with 'no sense of shame or modesty', deliberately exposed themselves to any female encountered on their march. In order to prevent this behaviour a local, Mr George Rouse, was contracted to carry them in his coach. Later military transport became available.[2]

The camp's function was to provide high-security prison accommodation for captured personnel from the Axis forces who were to be transported to American POW camps in the United States. It was an American POW camp, staffed by American troops, who were mainly not suitable for combat roles due to age and/or disabilities incurred during the war.

Whilst the purpose of ETO POW No. 1 was to process male prisoners, not all were soldiers or male, as one author, J. T. Thornton, recalls. She was asked to help strip-search two Russian women who were being processed after their ship had been sunk in a combat zone. She adds:

> Following the Battle of the Bulge, the camp was inundated by prisoners, some of them boys as young as 12 years old. As a result, two-man 'pup tents' [were] erected outside the fence that surrounded the camp, yet only one prisoner ever attempted to escape. He was soon captured and made to run back to camp whilst everyone else rode.'[3]

With the end of hostilities in May 1945 the tide turned and the Americans left the camp on 31 July 1945, with the British authorities taking over the camp administration on 1 August 1945. It was re-designated as Camp 157, a base camp for the reception of POWs returning from the USA and prior to their repatriation to mainland Europe. Whilst the camp had a capacity of up to 3,500 prisoners, there were only 1,284 at the time of handover, consisting of 1,205 Germans, sixty Austrians, six Polish and thirteen Czechs. Only two of the four prisoner compounds were in use, compounds D and F.[4]

German prisoners returning from American camps had been expecting to be transported directly to their homeland and most were disheartened and disappointed with their current situation. Many of the German prisoners being shipped back had been captured in the early days of the war and were still ardent Nazis. The American authorities had not imposed any form of political re-education activities and some camps had allowed the German prisoners to salute the German flag and pictures of Hitler. These men maintained their Nazism and held strong beliefs in National Socialism and Germany's innate superiority over other nations. Such men were now entering British POW camps and consequently the low morale and anti-British feelings became a great concern to the British Government.[5]

It was the job of Camp 157 to prepare these men for eventual repatriation but this was a task fraught with difficulties. The government's first and main priority, immediately after the war, was to its own people and to getting the country back to some sense of normality. The POWs were still needed to help rebuild Britain's infrastructure. Prisoners had to be appraised for war crimes and Germany itself had to be rebuilt as a democratic and stable country. These and other national issues had led to some criticism of Britain's repatriation policy.

Camp 157 was visited by Major Bieri of the ICRC on 17 September 1945, some six weeks after the camp was transferred to British control. The camp commandant was Lt Col A.F.B. Powell, ex-Indian Army, who retired on 17 June 1948 (*London Gazette*, 18 June 1948). The POWs within Camp 157 at the time of its handover had been processed by the Americans and now the British re-interrogated them, giving them a grading and new prisoner registration number.[6]

The camp leader of compound D was O/Gefr John William Till B30039 (previously 31G-22404), who was of American origin. His deputy was Uffz. Paul Landgrawe B175582 (previously 31G-5554). Compound D housed 665 men, with four officers, fifty-four sub-officers and four protected personnel (PP).

The camp leader of compound F was Hauptmann Hans Scheibelein B32590 (previously 31G-714524) and his deputy was Fw. August Barthlolmae B1591100 (previously 31G-206020). There were 619 men in compound F, including twenty officers, forty-two sub-officers and seventy-four protected personnel.

With the usual distribution of personnel it is of interest to note that of the 1,284 prisoners within the camp there were three civilians and only ten SS. Locals who were interviewed all reported that most of the prisoners were 'hardened SS', but this does not seem to be the case in August 1945.

The two camp compounds, D and F, were run independently of each other; they both had an office, kitchen, refectory, two toilet blocks, three washbasin units, a laundry, joiners shop, craftsman workshop, store hut, and canteen. One small infirmary could be found was in compound D and two more in compound F. The main camp infirmary was in one of the empty compounds, though the inspector's report stated that it would soon be used for all of the compounds. There was a library in compound F, which had some 300–400 books, but about 250 of them were sent to be censored and some of them were then not allowed. Seven boxes of novels etc. arrived from Geneva and these books had been censored.[7]

The prisoners were housed in Nissen huts connected by covered paths, with twenty-nine huts in compound D and thirty-two in compound F. Sixty men were housed in each double hut.

The prisoners had earned American dollars whilst under US control; this money had yet to be transferred to their British accounts, though the POWs had been given receipts for their dollars. Some unrest was expressed by the POWs with misgivings that they might lose what money they had earned and that the officers were receiving their pay first. Some 280 prisoners were allowed to work on sixty nearby farms, where some were paid 3 farthings (¾*d*) an hour, the others 1½*d* an hour.

The canteen was reported as comfortable and well decorated, but its stocks were very low and there were not many customers. Because of its low turnover it became difficult to afford to employ permanent staff. At this time there was nothing in the assistance funds.

As in other camps, church services were well attended and held in each refectory. The Protestant chaplain was Uffz. Albert Burghausen B30031, who chaired the worship every Sunday when 250–300 prisoners attended his service. The Catholic priest was San.O/Gefr Wilhelm Filtmann B30032, who celebrated services every Sunday with 250–300 prisoners, and also during the week when approximately 120 prisoners attended the service.

With the constant change of POWs passing through this camp there was little that could be done about providing organised educational programmes. In compound F, 115 were studying English and fifteen were doing literary criticism. On the social front prisoners were in the process of forming a choir. The theatre group had fifteen members and they built a stage in the refectory. The ICRC found that some prisoners had formed an orchestra with just two violins, one accordion, one saxophone (not in working order), two wind instruments and one harmonium. Apart from these events there were no cinema shows, newspapers or radio provided.[8]

As with other camps at this time, directly after the end of hostilities, sending and receiving mail between the prisoners and their families was difficult. In the case of Camp 157 no correspondence had been received since 1 August when the British had taken over, which had had an effect on POW morale.

A number of prisoner requests were made to the ICRC inspectors. The spokesperson asked for a football, a handball, some football boots and some books. The orchestra requested a piano, a drum kit, an alto saxophone and guitar, together with some sheet music. The education groups said that they would like some English manuals and some dictionaries. Finally, others wanted packs of cards, some water colours, and some oil paints, with paint brushes and paper to paint on.[9]

The Catholic priest, Wilhelm Filtmann, asked for some compilations of prayers and of hymns if possible and copies of the book of public prayer. Also requested were some New Testaments, rosary beads and some Catholic literature. The Protestant chaplain, Albert Burghausen, asked for some Bibles, New Testaments, and religious literature.

The inspectors made the following conclusions:

> The camp is very well kept and the prisoners are well clothed. They seem happy with their conditions except regarding the receipt of mail. Constant changes hamper any sustained activity and one hopes that this camp will soon be organised but in general it is a very good camp.[10]

The camp developed quickly under the British and all four compounds were occupied by 14 November 1945. The camp commander, Lt Col A.F.B. Powell, remained in charge throughout the camp's occupation.

Mr Haccius and his team inspected this camp following some complaints by POWs who had passed through Camp 157 and reported that personal items were being retained or lost. As reported previously, items were 'lost' – often as war souvenirs – causing a great deal of resentment amongst the prisoners. Again J. Thornton, one of only two civilian employees at the camp during the time of the Americans, recalls:

> Among the possessions taken from the prisoners I was shown the admiral's gold and onyx cigarette case handsomely adorned with a diamond monogram. I think it improbable that it was restored to him when the war ended; more likely someone still alive today has a nice souvenir!

At the time of Mr Haccius' visit the number of prisoners held had risen to 3,187 men and all four compounds were now in use. There were 903 in compound C, 729 in D, 848 in E and 650 in F. There were also fifty-nine in the infirmary. The Directorate of POWs (War Office) indicated that 10–20,000 prisoners would pass through this camp during the next quarter.

The German camp leader, now in overall command of the prisoners, was Hauptmann Hans Scheibelein B32590, but the four compounds were still administered separately.

The International Committee of the Red Cross sums up the inspectors' findings:

> We came to visit this camp to be given an account of the way in which this transfer operated, because several complaints arrived to us that personal objects were being retained in this camp.
>
> The detachments of prisoners in the hands of the American authorities are temporarily in cabins in a 'compound' of reception. The army registration card (Army Form 3000) and the attribution of a British number are done the following day.

A medical visit and an inspection of personal objects takes place, then, the prisoners unfit for work in the agricultural detachments and the patients are separated from the able-bodied prisoners.

The prisoners must present for inspection all of their personal objects (uniform, underclothing, documents, etc.), all that is not declared and then found during searches will be confiscated.

The individual record sheet of effects, clothing and equipment for working prisoners is established after this inspection and the surplus is put in reserve in stocks to be distributed to any insufficiently provided prisoners.

The valuable articles are withdrawn against receipts and placed in racks carrying the name and the number of the owner. These racks follow the prisoners from one camp to another, at the same time as the documents of identification.

The main objects of complaints were found to be related to:

1 Booklets of service ('Soldbücher'), these booklets are not stored by the American authorities before the transfer and it is not very probable that they are found after the many transfers carried out since the capture in 1944. A last step with this effect will be made by the American military authorities.
2 Identity Cards ('Sanitätsausweise'), male nurses and stretcher-bearers. These personnel often do not have identity cards and steps taken by the W.O. to obtain them are without results. Members of the medical personnel thus cannot profit from the advantages to which they would have a right.

We will try to obtain from W.O. that members of the medical personnel are recognised by the Americans after their transfer, same without identity.

The doctors have assured us that their qualifications had been communicated to the International Committee of the Red Cross at the beginning of the hostilities.

We have already attracted attention to the situation of the auxiliary stretcher-bearers to whom identity cards carrying the sign of the Red Cross seem to have been distributed in profusion by the Commanders of their units.[11]

These documents were very important to those concerned as they were proof of their medical qualifications. Being recognised as a medic or other related position by the British meant having protected personnel (PP) recognition with the associated pay and conditions.

Another POW concern was that they were only allowed to keep fifty cigarettes or the equivalent in tobacco. Any excess over this amount was confiscated and put on sale at the camp canteen. Cigarettes were used as a form of currency by the prisoners and any confiscation was deeply resented.

The doctors at the camp (Stabsarzt Dr Hans Bechre B59109, Stabsarzt Dr Gerd Radadloff B266188, Oberarzt Dr Karl Bochskaul B32605 and San.Gefr Dr Johannes LUX B266376) asked that, before their repatriation, in the absence of official papers, the ICRC representatives provide provisional certificates for those German doctors who do not possess their identification papers.[12]

Despite the POWs' complaints being investigated by the ICRC, the inspectors concluded that the administration of the camp was excellent, despite all the difficulties that often arose in transit camps. Only two prisoners had been detained, since the beginning of August 1945.[13]

The number of POWs being repatriated to Europe during 1946 increased considerably. In the House of Commons on 12 February 1946, Mr Maurice Edelman, Labour MP for Coventry West, asked Mr John Hynd, Labour MP for Sheffield Attercliffe, Minister for Germany and Austria Affairs and Chancellor of the Duchy of Lancaster:

> How many anti-Nazi German prisoners of war are available for the Oberon scheme for repatriating German prisoners of war; how many prisoners of war have thus been repatriated; and what steps he is taking to accelerate the repatriation of anti-Nazi prisoners of war in order that they may help in the reconstruction of a democratic Germany.[14]

Mr John Hynd replied:

> There are at present in this country some 19,000 anti-Nazi German prisoners of war who have been screened for consideration under this scheme. Some 2,200 have been selected as suitable for return to Germany. About 650 have been repatriated. Three hundred and fifty miners have also been selected for priority return. The Control Commission in Germany are ready to accept any number of anti-Nazi miners, bank officials, lawyers, factory managers, police, as well as experienced workers in agriculture and food processing, transport, post and telegraph services and public utilities. Repatriation of these prisoners is proceeding as fast as possible.

Mr Edelman then addressed a question to the Secretary of State for War:

> … whether he will now consult with the Chancellor of the Duchy of Lancaster in order to expedite the repatriation and release of anti-Nazi German prisoners of war, formerly at Camp 7, Ascot, and now mainly at Camp 157, Bourton-on-Hill, who gave useful political information and service to the prisoners-of-war programme of the BBC and who could play a valuable part in the reconstruction of a democratic Germany.

Mr Lawson MP replied:

316 anti-Nazi prisoners of war from Camp 157, who were formerly at Camp 7, Ascot, were repatriated on 7th February. A further small number of prisoners of war who were at Camp 7 will be concentrated for repatriation in the near future. Others who are at present actively employed at this camp will be repatriated as soon as replacements can be found.

Throughout 1947 the camp saw a constant movement of captured personnel. In May the total strength was 3,594 which included six Yugoslavians. Of this total 2,060 were due for repatriation on 4 and 6 June, and the ICRC report of 29 May 1947 states that a further forty-eight POWs would be leaving on the next transport.[15]

O/Gefr John William Till was now the camp leader; he had volunteered for the job and not been chosen by the men. The ICRC commented that 'He would not now command 10% support'. Apparently there was no other suitable substitute and 'Even a change of Camp Leader would not, in our opinion, be sufficient to improve the spirit of this camp'.

The POWs who were in the camp in May 1947 were housed in all four camp compounds, in double huts each capable of holding seventy-five men sleeping in bunk beds. The prisoners' origins were now mostly those captured in the Southern Command District. One prisoner was reported to have escaped and was still at large.

The medical staff were kept busy with some thirty-one patients being treated for a number of ailments and it was noted that two prisoners died of heart failure: Willi Schwarz D732132, a steward, died on 15 January 1947, and Wilhelm Dettman A974985, Zollsekretär, security, died on 21 January 1947.

The report indicates that there were now no POWs working outside of the camp, though there was a large number of PP, all of whom needed to be paid. Mr R.D. Dale of Manor Farm states that his father's diary recorded that the last group of prisoners came to work on 10 March 1947, with just one further POW on 30 April 1947.

Whilst the inspectors reported that the camp was well administered, the evidence presented indicated that there were serious problems developing within the camp. In the previous November, 1946, there was 'some trouble' between the British quartermaster and the interpreter officer. Both had then been transferred out, though the incidents warranting their removal were not given in the ICRC report. The compound officer, Captain Stoddard, accompanied the inspectors through the camp inspection: several minor requests were made and he assured them that he would report these matters to the camp commandant. One problem highlighted was that the POWs were not informed that they could dispatch one parcel every three months. They were to be informed the following day.

The final inspection by the ICRC took place on 11 November 1947 when it was visited by Mr E. Aeberhard.[16] There were 401 POWs in the camp with six in compound C, thirty-eight compound D, forty-two compound E and 288 in compound F. A further twenty-seven men were in either the infirmary or the administration block. Due to the nature of this transition camp there were 107 men on the permanent staff, all of whom were entitled to a monthly wage. This amounted to some £200, which was beyond the finances of the Welfare Fund. The commandant, Lt Col Powell, asked the London delegation of the ICRC to intervene at the War Office to see if some financial help could be given.

The new German Government, meanwhile, passed a POW compensation bill, which awarded any POW in captivity after 1 January 1947 one German mark per day. (This payment was increased to 5Mk for those still held after 1 January 1949.)

The postal situation had not improved in the last six months and the inspector was told that delivery was very irregular and no mail had arrived in the past fourteen days. The compound officer, Lt Stoddard, had instructed the post office at Moreton-in-Marsh not to deliver Customs forms and dispatch notes for sending parcels abroad to the POWs of this camp. This measure was lifted at the inspector's request.

The inspector wrote in his report:

> The inspection of this camp was fairly hard for our Delegates, because the spirit on both sides … is not what can be expected from soldiers. There is lack of unity and mutual understanding everywhere. One of the principal reasons on the German side is the outstanding (issue of) pay.
>   The whole kitchen staff was changed owing to food stealing in the cook house. Men repatriated to Germany have complained direct to the War Office, mentioning searching incidents and irregular disposal of contents of overweight kitbags.

Things were tense between the prisoners and those guarding them; evidence of this was the order by the commandant that no prisoners were to leave the camp before 3 p.m. Apparently this was a temporary security measure but was seen by the prisoners as another thing to add to their misfortunes. Many of the privileges given to the permanent staff were curtailed as a disciplinary measure against the prisoners. It is worth remembering that the war had been over since August 1945 and now, over two years later, POWs were still waiting to return home. The prisoners had access to newspapers and radio and were fully aware of the growing public voice for their repatriation as soon as possible.

Again the report singles out Lt Stoddard:

> There is definitely something wrong with the whole behaviour of the Compound Officer, Lt Stoddard. We took the opportunity to have a long private chat with him and tell him our humanitarian point of view. We believe that the conditions will improve in the near future. In any case the last transport has been fairly treated probably owing to the knowledge of the impending visit of our Delegate.

It also states that 'Lt Stoddard refers continuously to swindling and stealing, and imposes many petty and annoying restrictions'.

Criticism is also directed at the camp staff:

> To give an idea of this camp's spirit: a truck was sent a few days ago to the station, 4 miles away, to pick up the luggage of two POWs transferred to this camp. The luggage and the escort were loaded on the large truck, but the two POWs had to run the 4 miles to the camp! This was confirmed by the Camp Leader.

Whilst highlighting the many problems between the camp authorities and the prisoners, Mr E. Aeberhard finishes his report with criticism of the German POWs. He writes that Camp 157 was not very satisfactory:

> The German staff that stay many years or months in a base or transit camp do get bad habits, especially now they have the benefit of all the new privileges. A lot of bartering is done with repats, who have no money for buying canteen goods.

No date is given for Camp 157's closure but, given that the camp at Springhill closed on 31 January 1947 and also that Sudeley Camp 37 administration had transferred to Leckhampton Court, Camp 263, it seems certain that Bourton-on-the-Hill closed about the same time, early in 1948.

7

Camp 185

Springhill Lodge, Blockley

Springhill Lodge Camp 185 at Blockley, 16 January 1947.[1]

Springhill Lodge Camp, later POW Camp 185, was situated at SP 132 357 in the north
Cotswolds, located at the crossroads of the A44 and the B4081. Chipping Campden
and Broadway are just over 2 miles away and Moreton-in-Marsh about 5 miles away.
The camp eventually covered 7 acres of land acquired under war requisition.

The first ICRC report is dated 25 October 1944 when the inspector, Dr J. Wirth, wrote
in his report: 'The camp is one of the best fitted out we have visited. It was built by the
British Government in 1937 for workers' accommodation and the installation is excellent.'[2]

A fuller description was given by Mr Infeld and Mr Mamie six months later, in the
second ICRC inspection report of 25 April 1945, when they stated, under the heading
of 'General Description':

> The camp, as previously described, was already in existence two years before the
> war broke out. Many alterations and additions have since been made, and the new
> compound on a little hill near the enclosure will be opened in June 1945. There
> exist, therefore, many different types of huts in the camp; about 300 men sleep in
> the usual Nissen huts, 500 men are accommodated in timber huts of various sizes,
> the rest live in brick barracks. Gardens and allotments fill the space between the
> different huts; there is a parade ground and a little park inside the barbed wire.[3]

This report would indicate that there had been a great deal of expansion between
building the original agricultural camp and the fact that over 2,000 POWs arrived
during September 1944, just after D-Day and the invasion of France by the Allied
Army. In fact the camp is reported as having a capacity of 2,500 prisoners at
this time.

The actual events leading up to the establishment of a POW camp at Springhill have
not been established with any security and cannot yet be tied to any documentary
evidence. Campden and District Historical & Archaeological Society's (CADHAS)
current position is that:

> From local memory the camp was started about spring 1940 with a London
> firm Kirk & Kirk, who, using their own and some local labour, constructed an
> entrance off the Snowshill Road and made rapid progress building huts with white
> asbestos roofs. It is thought the camp was first used by a British regiment, maybe
> Worcestershire or Manchester.[4]

The current owner of the site, Captain W.L. Hannay, is quite adamant that
'The Americans came and put up the camp in quite a hurry'. Certainly this is also a
possibility as the American 6th Army Division with the support of the 86th Cavalry
Recognisant Squadron was stationed throughout this area of the Cotswolds from
22 February 1944 until their departure in July 1944. The 25th Armoured Engineer
Battalion of the US Army was also reported to have resided at Springhill Camp.

The American personnel numbers rose from 2,970 in May 1944 to 4,096 by July, just after D-Day, and this too would indicate a requirement for further accommodation. It would also explain the excellent conditions found in the camp. The accommodation comprised brick-built huts, heated by stoves. The kitchens were said to be well fitted-out with steam cooking, washing machines and other electric equipment. There is one other small piece of evidence found in the Moreton-in-Marsh Wellington Aviation Museum history pages. The January 1944 entry reads:

> … the WAAF's also started to meet the GI's of a large POW camp at nearby Springhill, who had a fine time teaching the girls to 'jive' and 'jitterbug'. The American camp was a whole new world to the visitors who were invited to partake of fresh dough-nuts, tinned fruit and other commodities not easily obtainable.[5]

Whilst the above account records Springhill as being a POW camp this is almost certainly not the case. The Americans were administering Camp 157 at Bourton-on-the-Hill at this time which was only a few miles further up the road. Italy surrendered in 1943, and some local accounts place Italian POWs in Springhill. There may well have been the occasional working group of Italians during the American occupation. Camp 157 was designated a POW camp under British jurisdiction and under the administration of the British Pioneer Corps.

The first recorded influx of POWs to the camp comprised 2,350 men: 1,140 Germans, 1,200 Polish, seven Dutch, one Frenchman, one Lithuanian and one Turk. The Polish contingent were members of the German Army but, given their nationality and superior numbers, were allowed their own camp leader, so that the first arrivals had two camp leaders: a German ROA, Gefreiter Wilhelm Biedorf, and a Polish officer, Lieutenant Tajtanowski. The Polish contingent is not mentioned in the next report made six months later when only Germans occupied the camp.

THE POLISH PRISONERS

Poland was invaded by Germany in September 1939, and the Germans subsequently invaded the Soviet Union (June 1941). As a consequence, a number of Poles, Ukrainians, Russians and other Eastern Europeans ended up serving in or alongside German Forces, whether as willing or unwilling conscripts. A percentage of these soldiers were transferred to Western Europe to help man the Atlantic Wall prior to D-Day. During and after D-Day a high number of enemy personnel who surrendered to the Allies turned out not to be German, even if wearing German uniforms; the non-Germans were sent to POW camps in Britain and elsewhere alongside German POWs, and this may explain the high number of Polish POWs in Gloucestershire in October 1944.[6]

Added to this, the Germans considered the Polish provinces of Silesia and Pomerania as ethnically German and all those living there as German citizens subject to call-up into Germany's armed forces; thus, although there were no 'Polish military formations' in the German forces as such, many German units would have a sprinkling of Poles. Most of these would either desert to the Allies when the opportunity arose or, once taken prisoner, would declare themselves to be Polish and join the Polish forces in the west. This was in fact the main source for replacing battle casualties in Polish forces in the west. In August 1944 the Allies took very large numbers of German POWs who became trapped in Normandy when the Falaise Gap was closed (as it happens by the Polish 1st Armoured Division fighting alongside the Canadians and the British 8th Army), so it is not surprising that in October there were large numbers of German POWs declaring themselves as Poles.[7]

The Polish prisoners that arrived at Springhill would have been given the opportunity to transfer into the Free Polish forces. Those choosing not to be so incorporated were sent to work for the British forces or interned in resettlement camps.

Whilst the Germans and Poles were treated alike within the camp they each had their own separate accommodation and kitchens, so that some form of segregation was applied whilst the two groups coexisted together.

The camp was well organised for the prisoners' arrival, as all the personal equipment that the POWs were entitled to was placed ready for their reception. Each man had two pieces of underclothing, two pairs of socks, one 'battledress' with green patches, one pair of shoes, and toiletries distributed by the army (brushes, linen etc.).

Because this was designated a base camp, no POWs were paid for any work they undertook within the camp. The prisoners were entitled to a 'special donation' paid on behalf of the protecting power by the administration for the first five weeks, but the report concludes that no prisoners within this camp had ever received any special payment. Since the prisoners had no money there was no canteen and so no build-up of a 'welfare fund' as described in other camps. The authorities of the camp had organised teams of workers to fit out the camp but this only involved about a tenth of the manpower and no mention of any payment is recorded. With so much leisure time on their hands the prisoners' only occupation was to build gardens within the camp or participate in organised social or sports activities. Of interest is a note from the report that states that the prisoners had sent 'their announcement of capture card' but at this stage were not permitted to write letters or postcards as the authorities had not yet authorised the men to give their address.

With the departure of the Poles and other nationals the camp numbers dropped to 1,583, comprising 1,579 other ranks and four officers. Gefr Wilhelm Biedorf was still the camp leader but now had two deputies, Uffz. Karl Dudek and Gefr Werner Nierhaus. There was also now a German medical officer, Stabsarzt Johann Siegmund.

The medical officer was supported by a British medical officer as well as sixteen medical orderlies, thirteen of whom were recognised as protected personnel.

Arrangements were in place to send any surgical emergency cases to the American POW Camp 232 at Northwick Park Hospital, with X-ray and laboratory work being done at a nearby British civilian hospital in Oxford. Later patients who needed hospital treatment were sent to the war hospital at Watford or Chepstow.

A GUARD'S PERSPECTIVE

Raymond Edward Watson, aged 19, served in the Pioneer Corps from 1944–46. Following D-Day he was posted as a guard to Camp 185, Springhill. Mr Watson, now in his 70s, wrote an account of his wartime experiences, which was published in the Royal Pioneer Corps Association newsletter in October 2012. The following is included with his permission and gives an insight into the role of the POW guards:

Springhill Camp was surrounded by parallel wire fences and guarded by four crude, wooden watchtowers. Inside, seemingly scattered at random, were a mix of huts of various shapes, sizes and methods of construction: wood; concrete and brick; and corrugated Nissen huts. The majority of these … were for the prisoners who slept 70–80 per hut in bunk beds, sometimes in triple bunks.

The garrison numbered about 100 strong and, apart from the Pioneers, included a mix of men from other regiments who were not rated fit enough for active service.

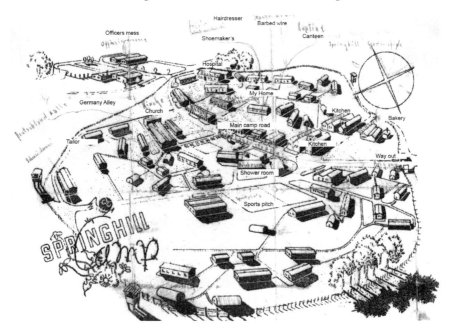

Springhill Camp drawing by German POW. English notations were added later.[8]

They were low-risk prisoners – not expected to cause trouble – private soldiers and junior NCOs from the Wehrmacht; and not just Germans, there were Poles and Russians who'd fought alongside them, I remember. This was my first sight of Germans up-close, the first time the enemy had a face. That felt a bit strange at first but you soon got used to it.

When new prisoners arrived at the camp they were interviewed by the headquarters staff whose offices were inside the main gate. I would describe the headquarters company as a cross between the Intelligence Corps and the Military Police; though I'm not sure they were either. Trained in interrogation and including German speakers they really controlled the camp and the rest of the garrison were there to support them. Although new prisoners were meant to have been pre-sorted, sometimes in these initial interviews higher risk prisoners – like SS and U-boat crew – were found to have slipped through and we had to escort them to another camp at Comrie in Scotland. We travelled by train, there would be 4 guards, usually led by a sergeant and a corporal, to 2 or 3 prisoners. Those were the days of corridor trains and we would secure a compartment and keep a watch over them … at least we were armed. We would arrive at the camp at Comrie in the evening so we would have to spend the night there. The camp was run by Poles, a tough bunch who hated the Germans, and we were warned bluntly to stay inside our hut until morning or we risked being shot on sight.

[POWs being transferred to other camps, whose trip meant an overnight stay, were placed in local police cells overnight.]

We weren't often in such close contact with prisoners and, in fact, guards seldom went into the camp except in support of the headquarters staff. Viewed from the perimeter, most prisoners remained distant, grey, anonymous figures, either massed at roll-call or in smaller groups moving around the camp. Roll-call, which happened three times a day before meals, was the only real structure to the day for those prisoners who didn't work; and many didn't. For those who did, there were some jobs based inside the camp, cooks and medical orderlies for example, but the biggest group were those who went out to work on neighbouring farms where they weeded cabbages or picked potatoes. I would often escort them, perhaps 3 trucks would go out in the morning, 60 prisoners in total, with a driver and guard on each. Only trusted prisoners were allowed outside the camp to work, we would drop them off in batches and only the last group would have a guard; the others were under the farmer's supervision.

I did get to know some of those farm workers. Many were friendly enough, spoke good English even, and were clearly relieved to be out of the war but others remained surly, uncooperative. You see, the camp was run according to a strict regime, low risk or not, and that could be a cause of friction with some prisoners who didn't like being told what to do or, indeed, being made to do it. I was threatened by one POW – told I would be killed if I ever set foot in Germany – but I didn't take it too seriously.

If there was wariness, distrust, dislike even, at times in the relationship between guards and prisoners it shouldn't come as a surprise given the war was still going on; but I am sure boredom and frustration also played a part in these tensions.

The guards' days were more structured but they could be very repetitive. Our regular duties lasted for 24 hours at a time starting around 6pm, made up of perhaps 30 men split into 3 shifts. The first shift would be out patrolling the perimeter or manning the watch towers while the other two shifts would be in the guard house just outside the main gate. One of those shifts would be sleeping; the other had to be more alert, reading perhaps or playing cards, and partially dressed in case the guard was called out. Each shift lasted 2 hours so you were effectively 2 hours on and 4 hours off throughout that 24 hour period.

I spent a lot of my time on duty patrolling on the south and west sides of the camp, close to a wood that bordered the perimeter, and in the watch towers which contained small, battery-powered search lights. At night these lights traversed the camp but otherwise it could be a lonely vigil waiting for dawn to break. My imagination had me wondering who was coming up the ladder after me because it wouldn't have taken much for a determined escapee to get out; the fence wire was well spaced out and we would have been quickly overwhelmed in a mass break-out as we were armed, not with a machine gun, but with just a rifle and probably 5 rounds of ammunition.

Escapes were not expected but there were some, though none were successful. I remember once there was a rumour of a tunnel but it came to nothing … most escapes were opportunistic and made by the prisoners who worked on farms. For those left without a guard it was simple enough to slip away if they wanted.

If someone did escape, something like a ten mile area would be sealed off with extra troops drafted in to help search. Escapees were soon re-captured as we knew where they would go. Those that had tried and failed to escape would be shipped off to a higher security camp.

When the end of the war came I viewed it with mixed emotions: I was relieved it was over but its end didn't mean either we or the prisoners were going home soon. Life in the camp carried on but, of course, the regime did relax. For one thing I think we stopped carrying ammunition. More prisoners went out to work on farms and a trade sprang up between the prisoners and guards for materials for the handicrafts which the prisoners made and gave away or bartered or sold locally. These handicrafts, toys particularly, went out with the farm workers who would offer us cigarettes and chocolate in return for the raw materials they needed. I know later some of the prisoners got on very friendly terms with local families who they often gave these handicrafts to but, during my time, the tension in the relationship between the prisoners and the guards never quite went away, despite the arrival of peace.

Raymond Edward Watson, 2012

 LATER DEVELOPMENTS

Gradually, as the camp developed through 1945, some prisoners did receive payment. It was reported that 360 men were in paid employment and as a consequence the POWs now had a well-stocked canteen where the profits from the 10 per cent NAAFI rebates amounted to £250 contribution to the welfare fund. The following prisoners were paid:

By British Army regulations — Tailors, cobblers and barbers, 20 men at 1s a day
Out of welfare fund — Cooks, tradesmen and staff, 120 men at 10s a month
As protected personnel — 13PP in infirmary, 30PP in camp unemployed, 43 men between £2 8s 0d and £2 16s 0d a month according to rank
On temporary working parties — 170 men, 6d to 1s a day
As officers — 4 men, pay according to rank

With so many prisoners unemployed and with a great amount of free time, the POWs had to devise ways of filling their days. They built a large and well-equipped stage where a variety of shows were performed. The visitors reported the existence of an excellent orchestra conducted by Siegfried Leistner. The orchestra consisted of twelve instruments, amongst which were two home-made violins, a home-made double bass and a home-made mandolin. The visitors were greatly impressed by two excellent pianists who gave classical and romantic concerts. In addition to the orchestra there was also a large choir, trained and conducted by Siegfried Leistner, who were reported to have reached a high standard.

> Furthermore, there are painters, whom we supplied with oil colours and brushes, there are designers, woodcarvers, sculptors, in many different workshops … Conferences and courses are also held, and an elaborate educational programme has been worked out.[9]

The YMCA, as at Sudeley Camp 37, were showing movies to the prisoners, which were gratefully received. The POWs were also allowed to read all the English newspapers and periodicals. There was a little library with German, English and French fiction.

Protestant services were held in the camp by a German soldier and Roman Catholic services were conducted by a local Irish Priest. The POWs of both denominations built a chapel in one corner of the large mess hall where Mass was said.

It is fairly obvious that the Red Cross visitors were greatly impressed by this inspection and, apart from describing the lack of any mail as 'deplorable', they conclude with these words:

This exceptionally large free time work programme, which is promoted and helped by the British officers to a large extent, creates a very happy atmosphere in the camp. With little work and practically no mail it is the only way to help these men to pass the time and forget their worries, and we were very pleased to see so many smiling faces and so much laughter, in spite of the fact that every single one must be greatly worried about his family.[10]

On 23 January 1946 Springhill Camp received its third visit by the ICRC. The inspectors were Mr Haccius and Dr Strehler, and their report shows little change. The camp capacity is given as 7,500 but the actual numbers are well below this figure. The maximum number ever recorded for this camp was 2,350 and that was when it opened in September 1944.

At the time of this visit there were 2,134 German prisoners but the report states that of this number 1,200 were capable of working, there were 115 protected personnel, 150 other personnel, and 650 incapable of working. No reason is given for POWs being incapable of working. The prisoners who did not work and were not paid represented a very heavy burden on the other POWs, and the ICRC representative Mr Haccius was asked by the German spokesperson if something could be done about it. The number of prisoners working as agricultural workers in the farms surrounding the camp was increasing and the local farmers appeared to be satisfied with this arrangement.[11]

The camp commandant was named as Lt Col J. Hassell DSO, MC, who was called out of retirement to take command of the camp. Reports claim that he was liked by the prisoners and encouraged their activities. The camp guards were attached to the British Pioneer Corps.

U-BOAT POW IN THE COTSWOLDS

Theodor Hunkirchen was born in Köln, Germany, on 25 May 1920. He signed on for the German Navy in 1939 (Service No. UN2806/39T) and in December 1943 he joined U-boat U-450 in Toulon, France.

The photograph on page 92 shows him wearing his 'pea jacket', sometimes referred to as a 'Collani', after the well-known German naval outfitter.

Obermaschinenmatt (Senior Machinist) Theodor Hunkirchen was taken prisoner by the British when his U-boat was sunk by the British destroyers HMS *Blankney*, *Blencathra*, *Brecon* and *Exmoor*, and the US destroyer USS *Madison*, whilst it was on patrol in the Mediterranean on 10 March 1944. All fifty-one German submariners were rescued and taken prisoner.

Theo was held at POW camps in America and later repatriated to Europe. He arrived in Antwerp in March 1946 and was transported to British Camp 2227 at

Cedelheim, Belgium. He was then transferred to Great Britain, arriving at Springhill Camp 185 on 14 May 1946. Ten days later he was transferred to Camp 37, Sudeley Castle. His POW number was N92807.

On 17 December 1946 Theo was moved to Camp 4, Scraptoft, Thurnby, Leicestershire, and on 4 January 1947 he was transferred to Cuxhaven in Germany. He was then taken by truck to Munsterlager, West Germany, now occupied by the British Army as a discharge camp, and then to Bonn for discharge.

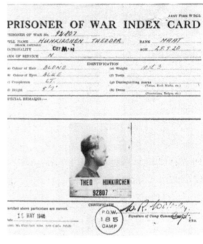

Theo's prisoner-of-war index card.

Theo (far right) on board his first U-boat, U-622.

Theo retained all of his service documents following his eventual release in Germany on 13 January 1947. His son, also Theo, later inherited his father's military papers and photographs (reproduced by kind permission on pp. 90–2), including his official POW forms.[12]

 THE FINAL DAYS

The report of the ICRC for 15 June 1946 contains a sad note that 200 new POWs from Belgium had arrived in the camp in a very bad state of nutrition. Two of these men died of marasmus, a form of severe malnutrition, on their way to hospital. Two others, Uffz. Erwin Ullrich 657432 and O/Gefr Werner Steinhöfel 315455, died of marasmus in the camp infirmary. It also reports the suicide of O/Sold. Wilhelm Esterbauer 31350, age 23 years, on 21 March 1946, though there is no coroner's report of this incident.

In June 1946 the camp had a German Roman Catholic priest, Johannes Muller A982039, as well as a Protestant chaplain, Heinrich EUCK B31367. A new post of studienleiter (study leader) was recorded and taken up by Dr Walter Alexius A816757.

Camp 185 altered its status when it changed from a base camp to a working camp in October 1946. Men were now taking on more agricultural work as well as road construction. With the Italian soldiers being repatriated throughout the country in early 1946, the German POWs found themselves replacing the Italian workforce. In April fifteen Italian workers at RAF Moreton-in-Marsh were replaced by forty Germans, with another fifty sent in June.[13]

The correspondence situation was still presenting some difficulties though it had improved overall. Letters sent to the American zone, particularly in Upper Bavaria, were often returned unopened. Delivery of letters sent to the British, French and Russian zones was said to be very good and, with the exception of Upper Bavaria, the American zone was graded as good.

One German soldier, Helmuth Rosse B552587, wrote to Frau Dr Eva Theuring in the German-British zone. He sends her his good news as:

Dear Mrs Theuring,   Springhill 16-02-47
Although I have not yet heard from you, I would not like to leave you waiting any longer.

Today I am in the unbelievably happy position to be able to give you long awaited information. I have known for about 1 week now that I will be repatriated next Thursday.

This knowledge has given me back an indescribable feeling of happiness, which has been missing for many years. Nevertheless I know that many weeks will pass before I can fully enjoy my regained freedom in this time of sorrow. In any case at least I now know where I stand and as soon as I am home again, I will write you a more detailed letter.

Please do not pay too much attention to the quality of my writing as this is due to the paper. With this I mean that the paper is unsuitable for use with ink. This horrible potato leaf paper has caused me to curse on more than one occasion. Thank God when I never have to see the stuff again.

So for the last time I will leave you with my best wishes to you, your husband and your son and heir.

As P.W your Helmuth Rosse[14]

Mr John Malin, a local historian, grew up in the village of Blockley and as a young man worked with several German prisoners. He said:

I was the estate secretary on the Springhill estate only a short march from the camp at Seven Wells. An armed guard came with them daily Monday–Saturday. We had four POWs. One was the stockman who looked after the cattle, milked them and cooled the milk, which was sent down to Springhill house … One was a first class motor mechanic who repaired all the vehicles. Another did the dry stone walling and the fourth could turn his hand to anything. They were all very polite people who did not want to be involved with the war.[15]

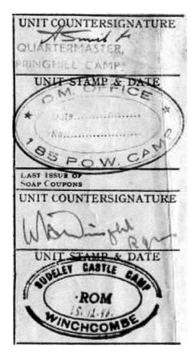

Official Stamps of Springhill & Sudeley Camps.

There were a number of changes to Camp 185 during 1947 as more and more prisoners were repatriated to Germany. In June the ICRC report by Monsieur Edouard de Bondeli shows a change of personnel, with the camp now administering five hostels and a number of billets. It also took over the administration of Camp 37 at Sudeley Castle on 20 June.[16]

The total number of prisoners was 1,872 on 1 June 1947, with 1,189 resident in the main camp. There were now five hostels that were being administered and for these the numbers of POWs were: 228 at Over Norton, fifty at Burford, 203 at Stanton, 123 at Condicote and thirty-nine at Horley. There were also forty POWs housed in various billets.

The final ICRC report by Mr E. Aeberhard was dated 10 November 1947, when the total number of POWs was now 1,186. The number in camp had dropped to its lowest at 673 prisoners. Of the five hostels there were now 185

Springhill Camp in 1950s, occupied by Polish refugees.[17]

at Over Norton, Burford was closed, Stanton reduced to only forty-five, Condicote increased to 181, and 197 in billets.[18]

The camp commandant was now Lt Col J.P. Fowler-Esson, previously of the Hampshire Regiment. His deputy was Major Blay.

As for the German personnel, they were constantly changing with camps closing throughout the United Kingdom. The camp leader was Fw. Georg Mueller 487701 in June but he was replaced by his deputy, Uffz. Augustin Bauer 816733, in the November report.

An interesting comment appears in the June report in that one POW escaped in late April. No name is given but the next report of November states: 'One man, mentioned in the last report, is still not back. He is believed to be in good health – at home!'

The official British view and popular belief was that nobody ever escaped from Britain. In fact a number of Germans had escaped from POW camps or hostels, many of whom did not wish to return to Germany. The official figures given in March 1949 stated that there were sixty-three POWs remaining at large and not accounted for. Several prisoners made their way back to Germany.[19]

Finally, Springhill POW Camp 185 closed on 31 January 1948 along with its hostels and also Sudeley Castle Camp 37, which it had been administering. (*See* Chapter 12)

Klaus Behr was a POW at Springhill from soon after it opened, arriving on 2 November 1944, and was on the last truck to leave on 30 January 1948. Because we know that he was resident within the camp until it closed, we can assume that he would have been one of the protected personnel. These are his diary comments:

31 January 1948

It's funny, but I still haven't found a good way to come to terms with my return home; for me, it is rather like the morning of Christmas Eve, when one is terribly amazed at how little 'Christmassy' one feels. Certainly it will probably be in the Munster Camp that the effective date of our immediate departure for Berlin will (finally) take place, which releases a rush of sensations in me. Yesterday morning we finally turned our backs on Springhill. The Camp had just come to the end of its own existence and had been placed under the control of Cheltenham [Camp 263 Leckhampton Court], and it was high time that we also departed, because the circle of old friends was thinning out more and more and thereby continually decreasing the 'feeling of wellbeing'. We also had the great fortune not to have to go first via Cheltenham with all sorts of uncertainties with respect to our luggage; we were the last to be despatched from Springhill, knowing that this would be the case; it breathed still of the spirit of our last, excellent commandant. So that was the first and the last that we had of Springhill, to which we owe so much and have so much to thank for.[20]

Klaus Behr

8

Camps 702/7 & 702/148

RAF Staverton and RAF Quedgeley
1 April 1946

Staverton Airfield, showing site of German POW camp.[1]

POW CAMP 702/7
RAF STAVERTON

Before the Second World War a small airfield existed at Down Hatherley, midway between the city of Gloucester and the town of Cheltenham, but in 1936 the councils of Gloucester and Cheltenham came together to purchase land for a new airport just across the Cheltenham road from Down Hatherley and named it Staverton Airport.

With the advent of war the Royal Air Force took over the site as a training school for RAF pilots from 10 September 1939 until August 1946. The construction of the airport and landing strips took eighteen months and, whilst the airport could not be used for pilot instruction, training was undertaken at RAF Worcester, flying Tiger Moth aircraft.

RAF Staverton was an important training centre during the Second World War and it is also reported that flying pioneer Sir Alan Cobham helped develop in-flight refuelling there. The RAF finally relinquished possession of the airport on 29 September 1950 when it once again came under the control of the local civic authorities.[2]

THE ARRIVAL OF GERMAN PRISONERS OF WAR

With the end of hostilities German POWs who had been sent to POW camps in Canada and the USA began to arrive in the UK as part of their eventual repatriation. Those held in America were mainly at camps at Fort Benning, Georgia Roswell, New Mexico. A few had been in the UK all the time. As previously explained, returning prisoners had been led to believe they were being repatriated directly to their homelands and their arrival at English ports caused much resentment and hostility.

This influx of POWs resulted in a substantial number of prisoners arriving in the UK, and whilst their labour was in great demand they all had to be housed, equipped and fed under the terms of the Geneva Convention.

The POW Camp 702/7 at RAF Staverton was situated just inside the boundary fence of the airport beside the B4634 at SO 884 220. All the POWs were German and their new accommodation was described as: 'Pleasantly situated in Nissen huts on the perimeter of the airfield that had previously been used for the air crews.'

The prisoners arrived on 28 March 1946 with an intake of 75 POWs from the RAF base (No. 2) at Kings Cliffe. Four weeks later, on 25 April, the strength was brought up to 250 from the same source but twenty-five POWs were transferred to RAF Quedgeley. A further twenty-six German POWs arrived on 19 June from camps in Belgium.[3]

The officer commanding was Squadron Leader Lawson, who was responsible for the whole station; the POW camp formed a very small part of his responsibilities. Flying Officer (F/O) Taylor was appointed the officer in charge of the new POW camp and was made responsible for all matters relating to the prisoners. He had had no previous experience in his new role but the records indicate that he showed much initiative and administrative skills.

The camp staff were chosen by F/O Taylor. He selected as camp leader, Uffz. Ettmanin Hermann D353576, grade 'A', described as 'an excellent man for the job although rather young and of lower rank than usual' (Unteroffizier = Corporal). He was 29 years of age and had been a teacher in his father's riding school until conscripted to the cavalry in 1937. He was described as a convinced and active anti-Nazi with a pleasant personality but not a very strong character. Owing to his lower ranking he was resented by some of the more senior German NCOs.

The POWs in other positions of responsibility had, according to the report, been carefully selected.[4]

The new camp was visited by Mr A.T. Duff of the COGA on 18–20 June 1946 to screen and card-index the whole camp and to prepare a re-education report.

The German POWs were graded in light of their political views about the Nazis, i.e. 'A' (White) having no political leanings, 'B' (Grey) still some support, and 'C' (Black) remaining pro-Nazi. The POWs were graded as follows: five 'A', nineteen 'B+', ninety-four 'B', sixty-nine 'B-', fifty-six 'C', and seven 'C+'. One prisoner remained unscreened due to the fact that he was away in hospital.

The inspector concluded:

> The POWs graded 'B' and 'B-' [grey] are mainly men who have been converted from blackness ['C'] by the extensive re-education carried on in the camps they were in in America. They state quite openly that their present opinions are based on what they were taught in USA. Those graded as 'blacks' were subjected to the same re-education but have resisted it; some of them pay lip-service to democratic ideas but at heart they admire Nazism in all respects and include some bad characters who have been trying to make trouble for those graded as 'A' whites.
>
> The few whites are men who have been convinced anti-Nazis for a long time, although they have been very passive; two of them are now beginning to propagate their views openly, notably the Camp Leader and one other who is trying to organise re-education.[5]

Of the 251 German POWs at RAF Staverton, 101 were working at nearby RAF Quedgeley. The inspector noted that these prisoners were being adversely influenced by the POWs at Quedgeley who were almost all classified as black 'C'. Steps were taken to stop this group from Staverton having any contact with these prisoners at RAF Quedgeley.

The COGA inspector, Mr A.T. Duff, was greatly concerned that no re-education programme had been instigated at RAF Staverton since the prisoners had arrived but reported that steps had been taken to get a programme up and running. The reason that there were no re-education activities at the camp was due mainly to the British staff being unaware that such re-education was both desirable and politically encouraged.

As far as other activities were concerned they had encouraged the prisoners in both recreational and educational activities.

A total of eighty-six prisoners were under twenty-five years of age and of these twenty-two were classified as being 'C' black (Nazis), sixty-two 'B' grey, and just two 'A' white. The inspector recognised that there was some very 'promising material' amongst this group and every effort was to be made to re-educate these men.

The POWs received a number of day-old British newspapers that had been supplied to the RAF officers' mess. Some prisoners reported concerns about the Russian political intentions after reading some reports from Germany.

No library books were available in these early days of the camp but the Gloucester library service had been approached and it was hoped that they would be able to supply books. The local YMCA also promised to supply some 200 books to the camp.

There were no films and no lectures provided but the POWs did have access to a radio. The set was fitted with two extra speakers and the guards reported that the prisoners had been listening to the broadcasts from the Nuremberg trials and this was having a 'good' effect upon them. The BBC was also listened to regularly.

Many POWs were engaged in English lessons and examinations in English could be arranged for those interested.

Other non-political activities arranged for the prisoners included classes in motor mechanics, mathematics and French. A group of twenty-two prisoners had formed a theatre group under the leadership of POW Daniels (B+) and all the material was written by them.

The spiritual welfare of the prisoners was cared for by the RAF chaplains. It was reported that the German prisoners consisted of 30 per cent Roman Catholics and 70 per cent Protestants.

Following Mr Duff's inspection and regarding exercise of the prisoners, a number of recommendations were made. These were mainly to do with the establishment of a re-education programme for the prisoners and included 'a supply of re-educational material for use of the theatre group'.

In order to stem the discontent and deliberate undermining of other prisoners, the seven prisoners graded as C+ were to be immediately moved from the camp.[6] (No mention is made as to where these prisoners were sent.)

The final inspection was made on 9 January 1947 and much had changed since the previous June. In September 1946 the entire POW camp was transferred to another RAF camp at 7MU (Maintenance Unit) Quedgeley.

Most RAF camps in Gloucestershire housed some German POWs; RAF Innsworth (very close to RAF Staverton) held 127 German POWs in July 1947.

German prisoners were still entering Britain, but by now in ever decreasing numbers. Staverton Camp was re-occupied by seventy-six German 'other ranks' with no officers in October 1946. The great majority of these prisoners were captured in Tunisia when fighting ceased there. In the words of the report:

These new POWs show absolutely no interest in politics what-soever and have had no form of political life at all since their arrival at Staverton. The Screening recently revealed the prisoners to be 100% grey and this situation has prevailed all along; there has been just no interest in politics.[7]

New POWs were arriving and the RAF personnel had also changed. The new OC was now Group Captain A.A. Newbury; the officer in charge of the prisoners was Pilot Officer (P/O) Rawlings. The German Camp Leader was Uffz. Willi Vollert (B+). It was obvious to the COGA inspector that the RAF staff knew nothing about the War Office attempt to re-educate POWs and they demonstrated very little interest in so doing.

The German Camp Leader was sick and a patient in Gloucester Royal Hospital at the time of this inspection and his deputy, Gefr. Willi Herrmans (B+), was acting Camp Leader. The 24-year-old showed very little understanding of politics or the necessity for re-education activities; he disliked taking any responsibility and lacked a good personality, according to the report.

The impression is given that the group of Germans who transferred to RAF Quedgeley in September must have taken all resources with them as this new group had no facilities at all. There were no newspapers, wireless, library, lectures, films, as well as no entertainment, and the prisoners were well aware of the facilities available at other POW camps.

Over 50% of these prisoners were under the age of 25 with no interest whatsoever in any discussion about politics. There were no prisoners in the camp capable of organising any re-education activity. The RAF Staff were unable to do very much but were co-operative and would help if outside assistance and material were forthcoming. The entire prisoner population was very apathetic and concerned only with their personal affairs and grievances.

Given these circumstances the general morale of the prisoners was seen as very poor. Temporary factors such as the non-issue of bonus cigarettes and the lack of a camp barber became issues that the prisoners complained about. Whilst these problems were being addressed by the British personnel, the prisoners assumed that nothing was being done.

Facilities in the camp are very poor as compared with neigh-bouring camps, and POWs knowing this, feel a sense of grievance. Efforts are being made to improve conditions, but results are being achieved only slowly. There has been no repatriation from this camp yet – the screening was only carried out very recently.[8]

The recommendations from the COGA inspector centred on the provision of re-education, including bringing in a German POW who had been on the training course as well as providing a library and films.

This was the last report on the camp at Staverton. Given the government's desire to increase the number of prisoners being repatriated, it may well be that these POWs were transferred out and the camp closed soon after this inspection report.

POW CAMP 702/148
RAF QUEDGELEY

In 1939 some 551 acres of land at Quedgeley in Gloucestershire were acquired by the Air Ministry for an RAF maintenance unit. This maintenance unit was one of seven such units built in preparation for the Second World War and it opened on 15 April 1939. The depot quickly took shape and storage units were built over eight different sites on the base. Soon after the establishment of this maintenance unit staff houses were constructed east of the main road, the A38 in Quedgeley, and to the north of Naas Lane.[9]

Mr Duff, on behalf of the COGA, was invited to inspect the POW camp at RAF 7MU by the RAF Commandant, Group Captain J.R. Brown, on 5/6 June 1946. This visit was made just prior to his visit to Camp 702/7 at RAF Staverton.

The commandant had requested the visit as a matter of urgency and Mr Duff's report states:

> He [the commandant] has had no previous experience of handling German POWs and has no staff for dealing with this camp beyond an RAF Compound Officer who does not speak German; the only interpreter available was L.A.C. Latham, a young man of German origin who has had no previous experience of such work. There were reports from the Compound Officer that there was political trouble brewing and the Commandant was very anxious to take immediate steps to prevent it coming to a head.[10]

Mr Duff made a full investigation of the commandant's concerns and all the prisoners were screened at this visit to establish their political category.

This camp was established on 1 April 1946 and the first group of POWs arrived just two weeks later. These were made up of twenty-four Germans who had arrived from camps in America and a further 150 men from camps in Canada, mainly Camp No. 133 at Lesbridge, Canada. None of these 174 men had been screened, although the commandant had been informed by the RAF base camp at Kings Cliffe that all the prisoners being sent to him were of a grade equivalent to Italian cooperators.

The camp leader was Fw. Emil Gebhardt; he was 32 years old, a professional soldier since 1935 and graded B+. Mr Duff records that 'he was not a good type and rather opportunistic. He had no personality for dealing with those graded as C 'blacks' of whom he was rather afraid.'

The deputy camp leader appointed at the time of the visit, Fw. Heinrich Schreiber, was 30 years old, grade B+. 'Good Personality. Has the right outlook but lacks political background. He wishes eventually to take lead in camp re-education. He was recommended for a political teaching course at Wilton Park, Beaconsfield.'

The interpreter was Gefr Klaus Groothof, 24 years old and graded B+. He was a student of electrotechnics before the war and had the right outlook. He too was to be recommended for Beaconsfield.

The screening undertaken by Mr Duff found that most were very 'black'. There were: two 'A', four 'B+', twelve 'B', twenty-nine 'B-', eighty-nine 'C', and thirty-eight 'C+'. All the 'C' and 'C+' POWs were from Canada and had been captured in the early days of the war up to and including the fighting in Tunisia. Many were men from the 'Afrika Korps' but there was a fair number of Luftwaffe and U-boat personnel amongst them.

> These POWs, almost without exception, have retained the arrogant and aggressive spirit of Germany in those days. Their mental outlook is still that of 1940; incapable of grasping the present situation they try to escape from it by the outright rejection as propaganda of all information given them by press and radio. They are forced to admit that Germany had lost the war but they attribute this solely to treachery on the part of the Generals; they feel important and frustrated and seek relief in the expression of an almost ferocious desire to get back to Germany and rectify the situation by sheer force.[11]

The prisoners graded 'C' did admit the responsibility of National Socialism for the war and its consequences but the prisoners graded as 'C+' were still intensely loyal to Hitler; they were almost all under the age of 30. Interestingly the two prisoners graded as 'A', white, were two young men who had rejected National Socialism on the grounds of their religious beliefs.

Those POWs graded as 'black' were very concerned about the Russian occupation of their country, especially Communism, and had a general lack of any understanding as to what Communism actually was. Mr Duff explains that 'their talk is that of anarchists prepared to wantonly reject or destroy anything they do not understand'.

The political trouble that Group Captain J.R. Brown was aware of was found to be due mainly to mixing, in the same Nissen hut, a small group of German POWs from previous captivity in Canada with others who had been held in America. There were two C+ (black) prisoners amongst the six from Canada who were reported to be expressing their views in a very loud-mouthed manner, particularly against any prisoner who was prepared to cooperate with the British. The hut leader, POW Gloc, was singled out and threats made against him, and his orders were completely disregarded. Gloc did report the matter to the unofficial interpreter and the camp leader but nevertheless resigned from his post as hut leader. The camp leader himself was afraid of the attitude of the Germans from Canada, seen as troublemakers, and subsequently did very little to quieten things down. Another prisoner from the Canada cohort, Heinrich Schreiber, grade B+ (grey), who understood the situation and had the personality to cope with it, was appointed deputy camp leader with a view to obtaining better discipline amongst his colleagues from the Canadian POW camp.

Mr Duff recommended to the camp commandant that the thirty-eight C+ (black) POWs be immediately removed from Quedgeley. (He does not say where they should be sent to.)

When Mr Duff visited the camp again on 27/28 August 1946, there had been considerable improvements noted. All the recommendations for improvement had been met by Commandant Group Captain J.R. Brown, with the thirty-eight C+ prisoners having been removed from the camp.

He notes that the 250 POWs at RAF Staverton were to be transferred to RAF Quedgeley on 15 September and the Staverton camp closed down. To cater for this increase in the POW population, new Nissen huts were built at RAF Quedgeley.

> On completion of this move the present Camp Leader at Quedgeley [Fw. Gebhardt] will be relieved of his post and the Camp Leader of Staverton, Fw. Daniels (B+), is to become leader of the new, larger camp. POW Daniels is a much better man than the present Quedgeley Camp Leader and shows a better appreciation of the aims of re-education. Other staff will remain unchanged.

The removal of the 'bad black' element had been met with approval by the rest of the prisoners and there was a noticeable change in their attitude. Whilst many were now taking a lively interest in the news and related politics, estimates of the political divisions were given as 10 per cent white, 60 per cent grey and 30 per cent black. Apparently one of the significant events to temper ideals was the broadcasting and thus revelations from the Nuremberg trials, which the prisoners could now hear on the radio.

POWs Klaus Groothof and Heinrich Schreiber had been sent on the fourth course held at Wilton Park, Beaconsfield, and had just returned. Their attendance on this six-week course saw an immediate increase in the re-educational activities of the camp.

Wilton Park had been set up by the Foreign Office to run courses to re-educate German POWs in an attempt to help them to think for themselves. Many young Germans had spent their entire life being indoctrinated by the Nazis. Military rank was not recognised within Wilton Park and the philosophy was to give mental stimulation and encourage the 'students' to return to their POW camp and organise discussion groups and re-educational activities.

In addition to the return of these POWs from Wilton Park, newspapers and a wireless were made available. A political discussion group was formed and 'A regular press review is planned as is also a wall newspaper and a camp magazine when the strength of the camp is increased. Great interest is being shown in these activities and progress should be good.'[12]

The first lecture, held on 6 August, was a great success, with POWs asking for more and weekly if possible. Given that the prisoners from Canadian camps had received no re-education, it was felt that this enthusiasm should be catered for with more lectures as soon as possible.

POW Groothof had formed a discussion group with a nucleus of seven POWs and it was hoped to expand this when the POWs from Staverton arrived. In addition to the discussion group, films were eventually provided by the YMCA and shown fortnightly.

Both English and French language classes were held in the camp. Two classes of twenty-fours beginners were held twice weekly for the English lessons, with another forty POWs studying English alone with books kept in a well-stocked library. One class of nine prisoners was run for those wishing to learn French.

> The improvement noticeable now is a reaction to the mental oppression from which these POWs, particularly those from Canada, suffered right up to their arrival in UK. In fact right up to the time of the removal of the bad black element, which had maintained this oppression, from this camp. The scorn and scoffing at all news which was so noticeable at the time of the last visit has disappeared and has given place to real interest. The one or two rather Nazi-minded POWs still left are easily dealt with by the majority of those who reject National Socialism.[13]

The final COGA report is dated 10 December 1946 and again the inspector is Mr A.T. Duff. Of interest is the fact that this report gives a POW camp number and type not given on previous inspections, namely RAF 702/148.[14]

The camp strength is given as two 'A', 174 'B', ninety-four 'C', with a further five unscreened, giving a total of 275 POWs all of whom were 'other ranks'. The number of appeals for re-grading was eighty-nine and only four POWs had been repatriated to date.

The key RAF personnel consisted of the officer commandant, Group Captain J.R. Brown, and Flt/Lt T. Adlard who was in charge of the prisoners. The German camp leader was now Fw. Arvid Daniels (B+), and his deputy was Fw. Heinrich Schreiber (B+).

The amalgamation of the two RAF camps of Staverton and Quedgeley in the previous September had been a great success in relation to the political progress of the enlarged camp at Quedgeley. There was a small amount of mutual mistrust following the amalgamation, but those graded as 'black' very quickly became interested in the political activities of the POWs from Staverton and in particular the two German prisoners recently returned from Wilton Park. The re-grading exercise established that there had been a considerable improvement since the last screening six months previously. It was now 6 per cent white, 89 per cent grey and only 5 per cent black. Four 'whites' had been repatriated.

It was now well over eighteen months since hostilities between the Allies and the Germans had ended and the morale of the POWs was noticeably low. They were feeling depressed at what appeared to them to be the slowness of their repatriation.

> The announcement that the repatriation scheme for the POWs was to be speeded up had the desired effect of raising the morale and the POWs indulged in a certain amount of fanciful thinking in calculating their individual chances of going home. They knew the scheme was working but to them it was not going fast enough, with the result that some of them were feeling depressed.[15]

The attitude of both the Germans and the British staff was all that could be wished for, and at this time the prisoners had excellent facilities for physical recreation, entertainment and vocational instruction. All of this was, however, of secondary importance to them and, while they appreciated it very much, their overwhelming desire was to get home as soon as possible.

Fourteen per cent of the POWs were under 25 years of age. Some of these had been a prisoner for over four years and were beginning to present a problem within the camp. They felt that their best years were being wasted and thus they showed a tendency to be easily influenced by a small group of malcontents. To counter this, the camp leader in co-ordination with the leader of studies, POW Bodil (B+), organised a series of vocational training classes. These were designed to teach the younger Germans the fundamentals of a trade in order that their time should not be entirely lost.

The extensive facilities and curriculum organised by POW Bodil in conjunction with the YMCA included the following vocational training that became well attended. Classes were held in the French and English language (for which the students could take exams and be rewarded with a certificate), stenography, motor-driving theory and practice, typewriting, and a teacher course. Fifteen per cent of the prisoners attended these courses and others attended a carpentry workshop and a metal workshop in which a forge was made available.

The COGA lectures held fortnightly were very popular, with up to 100 per cent attendance, and these were supported by a discussion group that was run by the camp leader.

The camp was now supplied with all of the facilities reported for other POW camps within the county, including an extensive library, newspapers and two radios, one for each compound. A request for the purchase from the welfare fund for a third wireless was made and this was to go in the 'Club Room'.[16]

There are no other reports found for either Quedgeley or Staverton RAF POW camps and, given the date of December 1946, it is quite possible that the POWs held in these camps were repatriated over the next few months.

9

Camp 142

Brockworth and Quedgeley Court

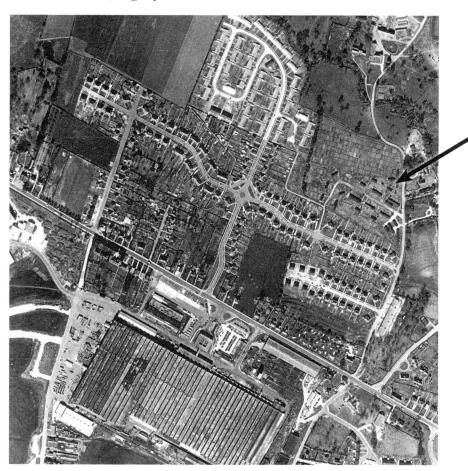

Brockworth area and Camp 142 at SO 890 168, 15 April 1955.[1]

BROCKWORTH

There are very few official records of POW Camp 142 at Brockworth and, whilst many of the locals could recall the camp as having been there, few could remember its location. The author has relied on a few oral histories from local people, correspondence home by Italian POWs, and one International Red Cross report whilst the camp was occupied by German prisoners.[2] Camp 142 is not listed in the English Heritage report of 2003 by Roger Thomas entitled 'Prisoner of War Camps (1939–1948)' but a search of the Internet resulted in several POW letters for sale from Camp 142 Brockworth. Several POW stories claim imprisonment at Quedgeley Court camp, also referred to as Camp 142.

A description of the camp at Brockworth in May 1947 states that it consisted of twenty-four Nissen huts including thirteen dormitories with twenty-two men to each hut. Also in 1947 there was a camp infirmary with twenty beds and a detention block.

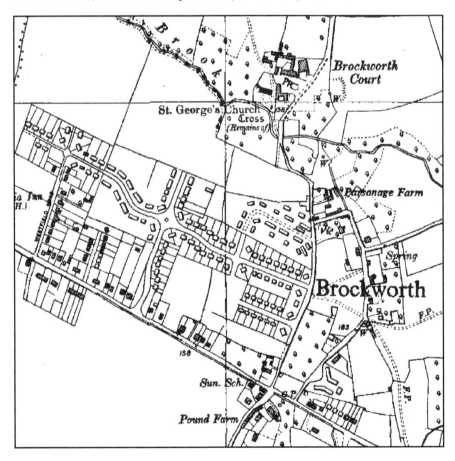

OS Map of Brockworth area. Scale 1:10,560. (*c.* 1954/5)[3]

This would suggest a camp population of just fewer than 300 POWs and the first group of prisoners to arrive were Italians.[4]

The POW Camp 142 Brockworth was bounded on the east by Green Street, which has now been renamed Court Road. On the north the allotments were the border and on the west it was Fairhaven Avenue. The southern edge of the camp met the back gardens of Boverton Drive.

During the Second World War, Brockworth was an important industrial area in Gloucester. Sitting astride the A38, after the Barnwood then Hucclecote road, Brockworth is the last suburb before the road leads off to Cirencester and eventually London. It was the original Roman route into the city. Immediately after the war large numbers of homeless workers arrived looking for work and shelter. A number of large camps were constructed to rehouse those families who had been made homeless and were looking for work, and displaced Europeans seeking refuge from a Europe in turmoil. The main centre of work was the Gloster Aircraft Company Limited (Glosters).

Glosters produced a famous lineage of fighters for the Royal Air Force during the war – the Gladiator, Grebe, Javelin and Meteor, and also manufactured the Hawker Hurricane and Hawker Typhoon for the parent company, Hawker Siddeley. Glosters produced the first British jet aircraft, the E28/39, powered by the engine invented by Sir Frank Whittle; its first test flight was on 15 May 1941. The first British production jet fighter, the Gloster Meteor, was the only Allied jet aircraft to see service in the Second World War.

The details of when the camp was constructed and then occupied by Italian POWs are not known but, like the others, it would have been about 1942. Several local residents recalled the Italians though little was said of the Germans. With the camp built close to a new residential estate, many accounts are from those who were small children at the time. One witness, born in April 1937, recalls that he spent his school holidays at his aunt's home just yards from the camp perimeter.

> I spent many happy hours playing around the camp perimeter fence and I remember that it was made of barbed wire. That didn't stop me and my mates from getting through it to be entertained by the Italian prisoners. The Italians were always cheerful and the most unwarlike people you have ever seen.[5]

TWO ITALIAN POW LETTERS HOME

The first letter is from Sergeant Giovanni Giunta T72394, who gives the camp address as 'I.W. Coy. Campo 142, Great Britain' (Italian Working Company Camp 142). It was written on 9 June 1945 and is addressed to his father, Sig. Giorgio Giunta, Via Grana, Modica, Ragusa, Sicily.

Italian POW letter. (Author's collection)

9th June 1945

My dear parents

I thought I would write and reassure you that I am well and I hope you are well too.

I have received several letters of yours where you state you had no news from me. You are right, in fact, I have been a little busy but please do not worry, this is because I have been working in England for over a year and I am doing quite well. Still, I hope we will be sent back home soon now that the war is over.

Please give me news of Pietro and let me know if he has returned home safely.

Best regards and a big hug to everyone in the hope we will be able to return home soon.

Love, Yours – Giovanni Giunta

The second letter is written by Sergeant Angelo Mancini T67990, Regiment H-R-M, War Camp 142. In the 'from' address he refers to the camp as a 'concentration camp' for war prisoners. The letter is dated 1 November 1945 and so he would have been made aware that he would be repatriated very soon.

To Mrs Di Lalla Vincenza, S. Croce di Magliano, Campobasso, Italy.

Dear Mum,

I want to tell you that I am well and I hope you all are well too. I have not received a letter from you for about 3 months and I wonder if you have been writing any or not.

No news here except they might send us back home in the spring time I think but please do not take this as definite.

Best wishes to the family … [illegible] and her family, a big hug, your son, M. Angelo. [6]

Mr Alan J. Snarey, who once lived in Camp 142 when it became a resettlement camp after the war, sent the author an email that read:

On Tuesday I attended a reunion of the 'gang' – we were a bunch of about 30 girls and boys who all lived in 4 roads around the Brockworth POW camp. From asking all of them present (about the POW Camp 142) all they could remember was breaking INTO the camp under the wire to talk to the Italian POWs who they say were very friendly. The Germans when they took over from the Italians were not so friendly. [7]

In another e-mail he wrote:

> From a friend of mine who now lives in Canada. He once lived in a house in
> Boverton Drive which backed onto the camp. His main recollection is of Italian
> POWs playing Volleyball all day and late into the evening as it was double
> summer time.

The repatriation programme for the Italian POWs started in December 1945 and
continued into the spring of 1946, some two and a half years after the Italian ceasefire
and surrender. No further records of the Italians at Camp 142 have been found.

THE GERMANS AT BROCKWORTH CAMP 142

The inspection report from the ICRC at Leckhampton POW Camp 263 for
May 1947 included Brockworth as a German POW hostel under its administration.
For continuity, however, what limited information on Brockworth appeared in the
Leckhampton reports is included here.

Brockworth Hostel was visited on 27 May 1947 by Mr E. Aeberhard, who reported
the following: [8]

1 The person in charge of the camp was Staff Sergeant Box.
2 The camp leader was Hauptfeldwebel (H/Fw.) Hugo Schumacher B196604.*
3 There were 184 POWs on the camp strength with 2 patients in the infirmary and
   a further 2 in the detention block.
4 24 Nissen huts including 13 dormitories. 22 men per hut. All amenities.
5 The camp leader stated that the food was 'in Ordnung aber etwas knapp für
   Strassenbauer', translated as 'all right but rather inadequate for road-builders'.
6 There were insufficient working clothes supplied.
7 The POWs were working for the Ministry of Works and Agriculture.
8 There were no complaints.
9 The camp infirmary had 20 beds. The Medical Officer was Ob.Arzt Dr. Anselm
   Lessman 523460, with one dentist and 2 orderlies.

The general impression was that it was 'a nice Camp with a very good Camp Leader'.

---

*   Regarding the German rank of Hauptfeldwebel (H/Fw.): in every German company
    there was one sergeant who was above all the other sergeants and his duty was to care
    for everything in his unit. The soldiers used to call him 'die Mutter der Kompanie'
    (Mother of the Company). In the British Army the equivalent rank would be
    staff sergeant.

Joachim Schulze recalls Brockworth German POW camp: 'I remember that Brockworth was not far away from Newtown Camp and I remember the theatre performance we were invited to.'

By December 1947 there were only eighty POWs at Brockworth and then eighty-four in March 1948.[9] As Leckhampton itself closed in May 1948 we can safely assume that the camp closed as a POW camp at this time.

Brockworth became a resettlement camp after the Germans left and Alan Snarey recalls that:

> My father worked for the Post Office all his life … they offered him a transfer from Marlborough, where we were living, to Gloucester as a senior clerk in the Telephone Manager's Department. Unfortunately there was no housing available immediately so we were put into the Nissen hut at the Brockworth Camp where we stayed for nearly 3 years, and then moved to a brand new council house in Gloucester.

 QUEDGELEY COURT

Quedgeley Court was offered for sale on Saturday, 14 June 1924 by Bruton Knowles & Company, who described the property then as:

> A most attractive Residential Property situate in the parish of Quedgeley about 2 miles from the historical Cathedral City of Gloucester with its stations on the L.M.&S.R. and G.W.R. lines, whence London is reached in under 2½ hours, and 11 miles from fashionable pleasure and health resort of Cheltenham …
>
> Hunting may be had with the Ledbury, Berkeley and Cotswold Packs. Gloucester Golf Links are about 5 miles distant, and the well-known Stinchcombe Hill Golf Links … are about 10 miles distant. Boating may be had on the Gloucester and Sharpness Canal which is within a few minutes' walk.
>
> The property comprises a well-built country residence with charming pleasure grounds, capital stabling and outbuildings, cottage, entrance lodge and enclosures of well-timbered park-like pasture land bounded on one side by a stream, the whole about 14a.1r.10p. [14 acres 1 rod 10 perch] in extent.[10]

Quedgeley Court was built about 1880 and from the property description was a large three-storey, flat-roofed building with much to recommend it architecturally. It was requisitioned by the War Office on 27 January 1940 and derequisitioned on 27 August 1949, when it was described as in fair condition. The estate taken over consisted of a private dwelling, garden, kitchen garden, orchard, field, stable yard and buildings in 14¼ acres. The accompanying lodge and a further cottage on the main A38 were not requisitioned.

Quedgeley Court, 15 March 1944. (Note the Gloucester-Sharpness Canal.)[11]

A lot of work was done on the buildings which were later used as a POW camp known as Camp 142 (the same number as Brockworth Camp). When it was given back to its owner, Herbert Sessions, who was then living at The Grey Cottage in Painswick, a total of 386 items were identified by Bruton Knowles & Co. as needing repair, and they produced an estimate of £4,010 15s 0d in compensation. The repairs included many items, but of interest were the removal of three lavatory basins and piping etc., and the restoration of the stables that had been converted into a mess room.

Quedgeley News produced an article entitled 'A History of the RAF in World War 2', where they state that:

> In addition to the RAF Regiment that was stationed there it had its share of 'visitors', German and 270 Italian prisoners of war were also detained with 'free accommodation' at Quedgeley Court and 'helped out' at the base.[12]

No inspection reports of Quedgeley Court Camp 142 have been found and certainly no reports on any Italian prisoners resident, with the above exception. There are several accounts of German occupation of the site.

In a House of Commons debate on the 'Prisoners of War' on 28 January 1947, Mr Thomas Skeffington-Lodge (Speaker) asked the Secretary of State for War for what reason the commandant responsible for the prisoners of war living at Quedgeley Court Hostel, Gloucester, has made the town out of bounds although it was within a 5-mile radius of their quarters, and has also forbidden them to go into any church, unless in an organised group, on a Sunday morning.

Mr Frederick Bellenger (Labour, Secretary of State for War) responded:

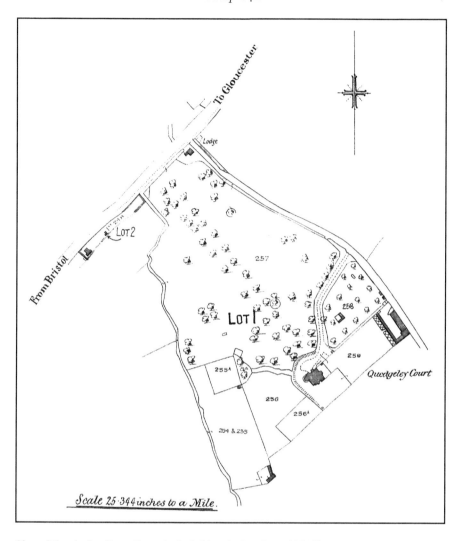

Plan of Quedgeley Court Estate included in sales brochure, 1924.[13]

Gloucester has been put out of bounds to all German prisoners of war in that area as the privilege of walking unescorted in the town has been abused. As a result of this order prisoners of war have only been allowed to attend church services in organised groups.[14]

No explanation as to the restriction on the German movement is given or reported in the local Gloucester newspaper but such restrictions were not unusual. One female witness who remains anonymous informed me that she used to fraternise with the Germans attending church services in Southgate Street, Gloucester.

Quedgeley Court (arrowed) in June 1959 showing a caravan park and new roundabout.[15]

Wilhelm (Willy) Reuter was held in a number of Gloucestershire POW camps including Quedgeley Court, and his story is given in part here as his experiences enhance some of the issues reported in the research for this book.

Willy was born on 22 November 1919 and became a POW, number 659302, in January 1945 until his eventual repatriation in May 1948. He was captured on the night of 20 January 1945 after serving six years with the German Army. He records:

> I was captured, surrounded by tanks on a farm in Zetten, near Nijmegen, Holland. I was searched and my weapons were taken, unfortunately my beautiful camera too. After many interrogations in different camps I was sent to a camp, a former cement factory, near Turnhout, a few miles from Antwerp, Belgium. In the Zanvoorde camp were approx. 6,000 prisoners who were under chaotic circumstances prepared for the transportation to England.

Willy's story shows the build-up of the German captives some six months after the Allied invasion of 6 June 1944. Also noted is his recollection of his property (a camera) being confiscated never to be seen again. On 8 March 1945 he was transported to England.

Embarkation in many small boats began on 8-3-1945. After arrival in England we were transported over three days in railway goods wagons and lorries to Hampton Park, London. We were accommodated in tents. Polish officers questioned us several times. Here I was given my prisoner's number – No. 659302 – together with my release number No. 26 which predicted a longer stay on the Island.

Transferred via two camps in northern England, he eventually arrived at Springhill Camp 185 on 10 July 1945. Here he reports that:

Food rations in all the camps were in short supply and guarding very strict. After a while the prisoners were used for farm work. Now for the first time we had contact with the English population: my school English helped a lot. On the big farm of Richard Wagner I met a girl who very kindly organised a dictionary for me which helped me a great deal during my imprisonment. I still use it today.

After about a year and a quarter I was allowed to write home for the first time. The answer, restricted to only 25 words, relieved me as I learned that my relatives at home, now in the Russian zone, were still alive.

To ease boredom in camp I needed a pocket knife to make toys. [His family owned a toy-making business.] A nice English man helped me. The rest of the materials for creating toys were somehow got together. The toys were very popular and I even made a little money which was forbidden for us prisoners. At a body search they found half a crown on me. After that I was no longer allowed to work on the farm. A white lie, when questioned by an English officer, secured me after 10 days not the usual confinement but a transfer to Gloucester-Quedgeley-Court Hostel (No.142).

As Willy Reuter states, prisoners found with money on them were normally given detention but he is transferred to Quedgeley Court POW Camp 142 in Gloucester on 23 March 1946. He was there for less than three weeks before he was again breaking the camp rules.

Willy Reuter (second from left) with young Patrick Barrett at Upper Hill Farm.

Here we had to stay in camp. We overcame boredom with nightly break-outs. On one of these I met a nice English girl whom I met frequently thereafter – always at night. When the German camp foreman heard of this I was transferred on.

He arrived at the hostel in Newtown near Ashchurch, Tewkesbury, on 12 April 1946 and moved into the same hut as Joachim Schulze.

Here I was able to work with nine other men in a flour mill under a Mr Healing. Our main occupation was painting. In the small carpenter's workshop within the firm I found an opportunity to make more toys.

On weekends we were allowed to leave the camp from 10.00-18.00 in a radius of 6km. Through some good connections I managed to get a bicycle with which I made tours for up to 20km on weekends.

At Newtown the POWs were allowed far more freedom of movement, especially over the weekends, and this confirms the account given by his friend Joachim Schulze, a fellow prisoner. (*See* Chapter 4)

Willy remained in the hostel for the next year and, as the prisoner repatriation gained momentum, he was transferred along with the other hostel dwellers to the administration camp No. 37 at Sudeley Castle in Winchcombe.

Willy Reuter worked on a number of farms during his wait to go home, making lifelong friends and eventually working at Upper Hill Farm on Cleeve Common from 18 July 1947. It was here that he met a young boy named Patrick Barrett, who befriended him and would eventually record Willy's story as a POW in Gloucestershire.

Mr Barrett fetched me to his farm after I had worked there a few times. He said, 'Willy belongs to my family.' His two children Heather (8 years) and Patrick (5 years) were good playmates and friends for me. Of course I made more toys. Even after 60 years Patrick's family, the children and me are still good friends.

My release number 26 moved slowly nearer and after three and a quarter years as a prisoner of war I was discharged home.[16]

POWs in Gloucestershire were repatriated via another POW Camp 263 in Leckhampton and Willy arrived back in Germany on 25 May 1948.★

As for Quedgeley Court, it was used for a little while after the war by the Women's Land Army who finally left the premises on 6 August 1949.[17] Eventually the property was demolished and replaced by a caravan park.

★ When Joachim Schulze became aware that I had found Willy Reuter's story, recorded by Patrick Barrett, he asked me to try to find his old comrade. After several enquiries I eventually made contact with Patrick Barrett and enquired after Willy on Joachim's behalf. Patrick informed me that sadly Willy died just a few years ago.

10

Camp 1009

Northway Camp, Ashchurch, near Tewkesbury

Northway Camp, SO 924 338, 18 October 1943.[1]

Northway POW Camp 1009 was situated in the grounds of what was once part of the Northway House Estate in the parish of Ashchurch near Tewkesbury. When offered for sale on Saturday, 10 June 1911 it comprised just over 25 acres of land including three cottages, pastoral land and an orchard. The house was eventually sold for £8,000 to Mrs A.E.B. Fair. It was described as a modern gable-ended residence of stone containing four reception rooms, sixteen bedrooms and dressing rooms, bath room and excellent offices, enhanced lodge, stabling and farm buildings.[2] Today it is known as The Northway public house.

Northway House and its estate were requisitioned or compulsorily purchased by the War Office in 1942.

An article in the *Cheltenham Chronicle & Gloucestershire Graphic* on Saturday, 10 October 1942 stated that after many years of residency at Northway House, Mrs A.E.B. Fair was 'obliged' to move from her beautiful home and gardens and has taken Twyning Park. It would seem, therefore, that Mrs Fair had no choice in the matter. As noted in previous examples of requisitioned property, such as Swindon Hall or Quedgeley Court etc., the War Office returned requisitioned property to its original owners when its use was no longer required and also paid compensation for any damage incurred, but this does not appear to have been the case with Northway House.

Between 1938 and 1940 there was a large army camp at Ashchurch and this became the Central Vehicle Depot of the Royal Army Ordnance Corps (RAOC), as well as the Royal Army Service Corps (RASC). From this the Royal Electrical and Mechanical Engineers (REME) was formed in October 1942, when the engineering branch of the RAOC was strengthened by the transfer of certain technical units and tradesmen from the Royal Engineers and the RASC. Major General Sir E.B. Rowcroft was appointed the first director of the REME Corps.[3]

The ATS were also involved at Ashchurch Camp as the female HGV drivers there were responsible for keeping the regiments supplied with their quota of imported vehicles, such as Jeeps and DUKWs arriving at Southampton and other docks. Some of these ATS women were also trained under Captains Bliss and Gosling in the REME workshops at Ashchurch to become qualified driver mechanics or fitter's mates.

All of these units of the British Army were transferred out to make room for the Americans and the RAOC were not to return until 1945.[4]

America entered the war after the Japanese attacked Pearl Harbour on 7 December 1941 and many thousands of 'GIs' arrived in Britain. Several thousand of these US troops were stationed in and around Tewkesbury and the surrounding Cotswolds. The facilities at Ashchurch were made available to the Americans and they set up a very large logistical base in preparation for the D-Day landings in France. Some seventy-seven different army units were installed at Ashchurch.[5] The Americans also took over Mythe House to use as a hospital for their troops. The base had a deep impact on life in Tewkesbury as a source of employment and social life during a very austere war regime.[6]

Northway House, 1911.[7]

Northway House, together with its estate, was given over to the Americans in 1942 although they had to wait for Mrs A. Fair's reluctant departure in October, and a large army camp was built for the American servicemen. The officers were billeted within Northway House and huts were constructed for the white American 'other ranks' near to Northway House. The black American soldiers were segregated to the far south of the site.

> In the early days accommodation was spartan. In August 1942, 3,000 men lived mainly in 'squalid pyramidal bell tents' while 158 buildings, including ten hangars and five small warehouses, were prepared. [These buildings refer to the Ashchurch military site.] A hutted camp was later built in Northway, possibly for the black American soldiers.[8]

History records that many of the white American soldiers were racist and did not get on with their black countrymen. Such was the animosity and violence between them that black and white GIs were not allowed to visit Tewkesbury on the same night. As for the recollections of local people, both groups were generally made most welcome. 'A black serviceman would always give you a lift in his army lorry.'[9]

Several American companies were based at Northway and Ashchurch, two of which were the 624th Ordnance Base Automotive Maintenance Battalion (624 OBAM) and the 622 OBAM. The 622 OBAM had originally been founded as the 126th Ordnance Motor Base Shop Regiment (OMBSR) on 9 July 1942. These units became collectively known as the General Ordnance Supply Number 25 or G-25. The 800 soldiers made the fourteen-day crossing to England by way of Fort Lee in Virginia.[10] For Ashchurch Camp: 'There was the vital extension of the Midland Railway line into the camp, making an extra signal box necessary to cope with the extra lines.'

Generals Eisenhower and Patton were frequent visitors to the Ashchurch Camp:

> General Patton also visited to inspect progress on his personal command vehicle,
> designed by himself, that was being fabricated by GIs at Ashchurch. Its basic units
> consisted of two 2-ton Dodge 4x4 trucks that were converted to one vehicle with
> much more traction and a longer bed. In its finality it certainly resembled the char-
> acter of Gen. Patton. The GIs at Ashchurch were very proud of this contribution.[11]

There were no Italian POWs at Northway although there were a few Italians at the
hostel at Newtown, on the present site of the beer garden of the Canterbury Leys
public house, as well as in a few huts opposite the current entrance to the Ashchurch
Camp. Italian workers were also trucked in from the POW camp at Sudeley. Both
Joachim Schulze and Wilhelm Reuter, German POWs, were held at Newtown which
was under the administration of Camp 37 Sudeley Castle.

A section of the camp was in fact used by the Americans as a POW Camp (G-25)
until it was officially handed over to the British on 28 May 1946; then became the
British Camp 1009. It is described as consisting of nineteen huts, which were dormitories (no mention of the Nissen huts). There was electric lighting and stove heating
throughout.

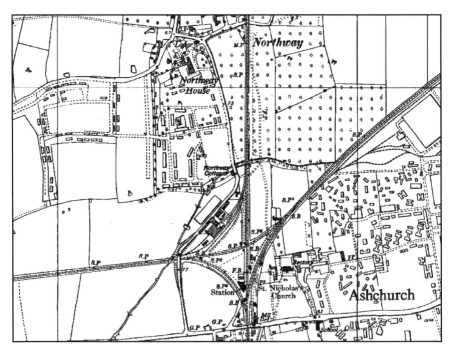

OS map showing Northway House and its estate about 1946, as published in 1955. Many of the
army and POW huts can still be seen.

Major R.A. Sweet (with walking stick), 1947. Also in the photo are three German POWs.

No documentation about the American-administered POW camp has been located as the US Army removed all records when they handed the camp over to the British authorities. One incident, however, is recorded by an inquiry at Tewkesbury Town Hall by the coroner, Mr J.D. Lane, regarding the suicide of Erich Jakubzik, a 32-year-old German 'Soldat'. A report of the inquiry was included in the *Gloucestershire Echo* dated 20 December 1945. An American Pfc Ulrich Handel was the interpreter at this inquiry.

Lieutenant Leonard M. Mason of the US Army gave evidence that Jakubzik had been a miner in his civilian life and was a POW at No. 1 Stockade at the camp. The prisoner had recently been told of the loss of his wife and children as well as his home.

Frederick Treppenor, a POW at No. 2 Stockade (this is the first evidence that the camp was segregated into at least two 'Stockades'), said that for some days before Jakubzik went missing he did not speak to any of his friends. While working at hangar No.6 at the Ashchurch military camp on the previous Saturday, 24 November, Jakubzik went away and was reported as missing.

On Monday 26 the NCO Hill told Treppenor to look for him. At 2.30 p.m., in company with another POW, they found him in a three-quarter-full water tank. The coroner reported that Erich Jakubzik had died from drowning and his suicide had occurred whilst the balance of his mind was disturbed.[12]

As we have seen in previous chapters, many Germans were being returned from American and Canadian POW camps at this time and repatriation of essential German personnel was taking place in order to rebuild Germany.

Conditions within the POW camps were being relaxed as can be seen in this extract from a debate in the House of Commons on 28 January 1947:

> Mr Sorensen MP asked the Secretary of State for War whether he will consider having the barbed wire around prisoner of war camps removed and also the large sized lettering frequently painted or stamped on prisoner of war clothing.

Mr Bellenger in his reply stated that:

> It has already been decided that in working camps the wire should be replaced by a token perimeter fence; this is still necessary to mark the limits of the camp and to discourage the entry of unauthorised persons. I am considering the question of the distinguishing marks on prisoners' clothing.[13]

Prisoner of War Working Company, Northway Camp 1009, Ashchurch, was inspected on 8 March 1947 by the ICRC delegates M. de Bondeli and his colleague Mr E.A. Aeberhard.

The capacity of Camp 1009 was only 800 men and as such it was a relatively small POW camp. The prisoners were employed at the Ashchurch logistical base. On the date of the ICRC visit the camp strength was recorded as 443 POWs, including three protected personnel. This number included one officer, thirty non-commissioned officers (NCOs) and 412 other ranks. The 443 prisoners were made up of 420 Wehrmacht Heer (army), three marine (navy), sixteen Luftwaffe (air force), one SS and three Reichsarbeitdienst (RAD or Reich Labour Service). All were Germans. Most were captured by US forces in France and Germany and they were graded as 250 'B' and 180 'C' (thirteen not yet graded).[14]

German Administration: the Camp Leader had a copy of the Geneva Convention.[15]

The camp commandant was Major Reginald Arthur Sweet 146318 who was given an emergency commission in 287 Company Pioneer Corps on 9 September 1940. He was taken on strength to 179 Coy on 15 September 1940 as a lieutenant, and was later transferred to 319 Coy where he was promoted to captain. From December 1944 he was with 326 Coy attached to the RAOC Depot at Didcot, until it was eventually disbanded on 25 July 1945. Captain Sweet was eventually promoted to major and then became commandant at Northway POW Camp 1009. He was born in 1890 and was 50 years old at the time of his commission; he died in 1960 in the Evesham district at the age of 70.[16]

The German administration was listed as:

Camp Leader: O/Fw. Gustav Siebert B174301
Asst Camp Leader: Fw. Leo Hoffmann B174500
Sen. Med. Officer: St/Arzt Ernst Rosenberger B174768
Dentist: San.Uffz. Ludwig Dittmeyer B174386

The ICRC report includes the 'bill of fare' for the day of the inspection:

Breakfast: Haferflockensuppe, Brot, Tee (porridge, bread, tea)
Dinner: Nudelsuppe mit Fleischeinlage, Brot, Tee (noodle soup with meat, bread, tea)
Supper: Salz Kartoffeln, Schweinswürstchen, Mais, Brot, Margarine, Kaffee (boiled potatoes, pork sausages, corn, bread, margarine, coffee)

A quiet place to listen to the radio.

The receiver in the picture on page 125 is almost certainly an S/SX-16 Super Skyrider made by Hallicrafters in the USA in the years immediately before the Second World War. It was an 11-valve superhet covering from medium waves up to 60MHz with a couple of 6V6s producing 10watts of audio output. This was known as a very nice set for medium- and short-wave broadcast reception, and the POWs would have had no problem in hearing German broadcasts. The receivers were imported into the UK in the 1930s and were used by the US Army during the Second World War.

The senior medical officer, St. Arzt. Ernst Rosenberger, and the camp dentist, San. Uffz. Ludwig Dittmeyer, were assisted by three protected personnel, comprising one infirmary officer and two other ranks. The daily number of attendances at sick parade was ten men. Those cases that could be managed within the camp were treated in the infirmary which had twenty-two beds in a ward housed in one hut.

On the day of the inspection there were six cases within the infirmary but none of these were classified as serious. Should any prisoner need immediate emergency treatment he was transferred to Gloucester City General Hospital. The German medical officer reported on the general health of the men as 'Ausgezeichnet' (Excellent), and that the general state of the POWs' nutrition was 'Sehr gut' (Very good).

The majority of the prisoners worked at the RAOC depot across the railway line in Ashchurch depot, which was reached by way of a metal footbridge over the mainline railway that ran between Ashchurch and Northway. This bridge, most likely constructed by the Americans, is still in use today.

The POWs' canteen was a very important building as it was a focus and meeting place for the prisoners when at leisure. Most commodities were made available and whilst the men received twenty-five cigarettes each week further packets could be purchased from the canteen. At the time of the visit the welfare fund stood at £35, which could be used by the camp administration to purchase items such as sports equipment for the camp's use. Of interest is that the canteen was built by using two Nissen huts joined together.

The German canteen – two Nissen huts joined together.

The interior layout.

The chapel at Northway Camp.

No COGA inspection reports were found at The National Archives at Kew but, as with the other German Camps, political lectures and visits to British council meetings, museums and other re-education would have taken place, as it was of great importance to the War Office in the de-Nazification of German POWs. No mention is made in the ICRC report but they do indicate that the prisoners have organised educational classes in English and French. The camp leader made a request to the inspectors for ten books on French literature for the POWs studying French. The camp library had 480 books in stock, of which 253 were fiction.

Northway Camp had its own chapel where a Protestant service was held monthly by a POW chaplain who came over from Camp 157, Bourton-on-the-Hill. A Roman Catholic POW came from Camp 263 Leckhampton every month, staying at Northway for five days.

Weekly services were held by Father Thomas J. Morrissey who was the parish priest at Saint Joseph's church on the Mythe, Tewkesbury, between 1939 and 1951.

German camp band (above) and German camp orchestra (below).

The sports ground with running and tug of war.

It would appear that the priest travelled by bicycle as the local newspaper reported on 15 July 1944: 'Wonderful Escape: Father Morrissey of St Joseph's Roman Catholic Church at the Mythe: forced off bike by skidding tank on Mythe Causeway.'[17] As if this were not enough, another report of 30 September 1944 reads that Father Morrissey had a 'second escape from an accident with US vehicles. His bicycle was apparently wrecked by an encounter with a US Vehicle but it was replaced by them soon after.'[18]

The camp had an active orchestra with nine instruments as well as a more modern band.

The German prisoners called their ensemble the Playing Blue Band or PBB. As well as the band the POWs had an active theatre group of fifteen players, and regular film shows were provided by the YMCA.

Four members of the band formed a group called the 'Chamber Quartet' and they gave a farewell concert for the people of Tewkesbury at the Tewkesbury Methodist Church. The leader of the quartet was named as Otto H. Krause, who gave organ and viola solos by Bach and Mendelssohn. Other members of the quartet were H. Muck on violin, L. Kramarek on viola, and K. Wallbaum on French horn.[19] The concert took place on Saturday, 31 May 1947 just before the camp was closed.

Like all the other camps in Gloucestershire, both German and Italian sports were very popular. Northway Camp was provided with a sports ground and football was

Northway Camp at Ashchurch, near Tewkesbury.

Northway Camp at Ashchurch, near Tewkesbury.

played on a regular basis. Games were often arranged with players from other POW camps and sometimes with the British troops.

There were no complaints made to the visiting Red Cross inspectors but the camp leader did request that re-screening of those POWs classified as 'C' be done as soon as possible.

POW Camp 1009 Northway, Ashchurch near Tewkesbury, closed in 1947 when the Germans were repatriated. The camp then remained empty with the exception of a few displaced people, before it became a new housing estate that remains to this day.

Nothing remains of the POW camp but the new estate, built around the old US Army base layout, includes Lee Walk, Virginia Road and Virginia Close. These are named after the US Army stationed at Northway, e.g. Lee Base was the United States Army base in Virginia, USA. The pedestrian railway bridge built by the United States Army to connect the camp with Ashchurch depot still exists.

Northway became a new parish in its own right on 1 April 2008.

11

Camp 327–232

Northwick Park, German POW Hospital

The Northwick House mansion and its estate, Northwick Park, were inherited in 1912 by Lady Augusta Northwick's grandson, Captain George Spencer-Churchill, MC FSA (1876–1964). Prior to 1931 the Northwick estate, which included Blockley village, was actually a small enclave of the county of Worcestershire and was surrounded by the county of Gloucestershire.[1] George Spencer-Churchill's cousin Winston Churchill, prime minister, held a number of important meetings there during the Second World War.[2]

Northwick Park SP 168
365, 16 January 1947.[3]

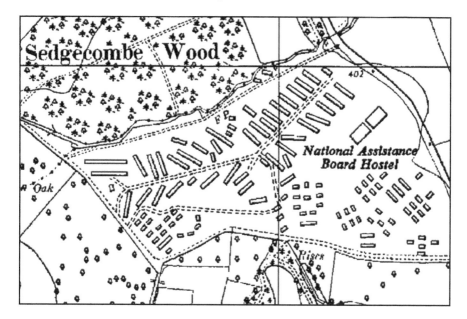

Northwick Park SP 168 365, 16 January 1947.[4]

There was a considerably large United States Army deployment in and around Northwick Park, Blockley Parish, Batsford and Moreton-in-Marsh during the war and leading up to the D-Day landings on 6 June 1944. The Norhwick estate and surrounding area was used by the American 6th Armoured Division and the 86th Cavalry Reconnaissance Squadron from February 1944. The 15th Tank Battalion with its 341 tanks was based at the nearby town of Moreton-in-Marsh. As part of the D-Day plans America instigated a number of medical facilities throughout the UK including field hospitals known in American terms as station hospitals. The 327th Station Hospital, USAFBI (United States Army Forces in the British Isles), was constructed in an area of Northwick Park by the reputable construction firm Higgs & Hill. Construction contracts were agreed in May 1943 stipulating that the hospital was to be completed within six months.[5]

An advance party of US medical staff and other army essential personnel arrived at the new station hospital on Monday, 20 December 1943 from their previous base in Iceland. There was then a short delay of two weeks before the rest of the medical staff and chaperoned nurses arrived by train on Tuesday, 4 January 1944.

It was noted in several accounts that the hospital chapel and the mortuary were still under construction.[6]

On Thursday, 6 January 1944 a meeting took place somewhere in Britain attended by a few women from the American Red Cross. The meeting was chaired by a Miss Kent, who informed Miss Esther Weikel (secretary), Miss Beverley Bates (recreation worker), and Mrs Augusta Noyce (assistant field director), that their services were required at the

327 Station Hospital in the Cotswolds of Gloucestershire. A report states how excited the three Red Cross workers were when Miss Kent described the beautiful Cotswold country where the hospital was located. They were informed that the Hospital Unit had been in Iceland recently and had only just arrived in England. The women recorded that they were expecting very harsh and primitive conditions and likened their expectations as 'characteristic of pioneering life'.[7]

The three American Red Cross workers arrived two days later on Saturday, 8 January and were pleasantly surprised by their reception and conditions. They were invited to Colonel Robert's office, the hospital commanding officer. Later that same day, they were greeted and made very welcome by the adjutant and executive officer, the chief nurse and Major Kasparian, the special services officer (and chief of surgical services). Major Kasparian then explained life on a military post and the channels open to them.

The women were shown to their new quarters, which were situated at the end of a ward and were far from the primitive conditions expected; they were met with a warm open fire and the services of several army personnel responsible for all of the domestic duties. A plan of what the Red Cross could offer to the staff and patients was drawn up. It was also agreed with the medical staff that, from the month of February, they would be responsible for the supervision of the dayroom during the hours used by other ranks as well as the hours used by the patients. The officers had their own mess and facilities as did other ranks and also the ambulatory patients.

Some insight is obtained about the 327 Station Hospital in these first few months from the American Red Cross monthly reports. They report that a very active and efficient special service department was already established and the sergeant responsible was keenly interested in the welfare of all the GIs in and out of the hospital. (There is no mention at this point about any POWs.)

The sergeant in charge was very talented, an ex-dancing teacher and interior decorator; he was very successful in Iceland and had won the respect of the colonel. He had brought with him from Iceland samples of the handiwork done there and hoped to do the same type of work here. He had ordered thirty-six radios, furniture for two dayrooms, two gramophones, and two pianos and over 1,000 books.[8]

There were a great many requests of the Red Cross women during the first few days from the enlisted men. Some were for general information about furloughs (a voluntary and temporary unpaid leave), others regarding army correspondence courses or how to locate relatives in the services. It would seem that their task, involving both staff and patients, was somewhere between social worker and occupational therapist. Their main remit was to participate in the rehabilitation of the hospitalised GIs.

Considerable time was spent with one young officer on the ward, discussing the army correspondence course and looking up material for him. Another boy was anxious about his trip to London and was quite apprehensive that he might miss seeing his brother whom he had not seen for several years. A cable was sent to relatives on two occasions when a patient's father died.

The Red Cross files show that the majority of the patients were black Americans, who showed a great interest in card games of all kinds. The Red Cross introduced a checkers (draughts) tournament between two wards with the winner receiving a 'Grand Prize'. Some difficulty was experienced in getting the 'white and coloured' patients to mix in joint activities and this is noted in a comment that 'we will need to take careful planning to include both in apt programs'.[9]

Initially there were few ambulatory patients so many activities were held at ward level, but medical approval was soon obtained for those patients that were able to attend, with any hospital staff off duty, the evening movies which at this time were shown twice weekly. The movies were supplied by Special Services.

The theatre doubled as a meeting hall and was made available from Sunday, 30 January 1944. The Red Cross started using the room as a recreation room and were anxious to decorate it in such a way that the 'men will really flock' to it. Both enlisted men and patients used the facility to listen to the radio, read books or write letters. By February all were awaiting the arrival of a pool table and a piano.[10]

It would almost seem that their needs (the enlisted men and staff) were greater than those of many patients. They had been overseas thirty months or more and had been isolated in Iceland, and they were somewhat isolated here. They had lost their spontaneity and seemed to be seeking for something to make life more satisfying.[11]

During the month of February a new ward was opened for American troops who were serving custodial punishment, and at least one-sixth of the hospital population was under guard. There was still no mention in the reports of any German prisoners of war though the International Red Cross reports from other Gloucestershire POW camps stated that several POWs in need of hospital care had been transferred to Northwick Park.

One of the wards was set aside for the treatment of venereal disease (VD) and was experiencing an increase in the number of patients that it treated. The patients with VD were confined to the ward and an estimate was made that in all about one-fourth of the hospital population was permanently confined to their wards. The Red Cross workers were allowed to work on these wards, though the use of sharp tools was not allowed on the prisoners' ward.

During February the patients' dayroom began to take shape. Ivy and greenery were gathered from the nearby woods and used to decorate the room, thus giving it a 'home-like' look. The plan was to turn it into a 'hunting lodge' and the Special Services sergeant went with Mrs Augusta Noyce, Assistant Field Director of the Red Cross, to find and buy some deer's horns and stuffed game from an 'astonished taxidermist' in a nearby town.

The patients' dayroom was officially opened on 19 March 1944 with a grand opening ceremony. The American Red Cross ladies and the Special Service Department had made what they interpreted as an English Lodge. It was painted mauve in colour and sported moose heads, deer horns and stuffed birds. They also produced rustic flower pots from logs found in nearby woods and attached hanging ivy to the walls.

An active programme of entertainment, film shows, trips to the local village and public houses were all introduced, as well as a monthly cake cooked by the mess sergeant for any patient having a birthday that month. Parties were arranged every Sunday afternoon. One report tells of a group of twenty-five patients visiting Northwick Park Mansion on 22 March; they were shown the many splendid paintings and antiques, with a trip around the extensive gardens, by Captain Spencer-Churchill himself.

A horseshoe court was improvised outside the recreation hall with some used horseshoes from a nearby blacksmith.

Miss Beverley Bates, the Red Cross Recreation Coordinator, was transferred out to the 30th General Hospital and replaced by Miss Verna Emanuel on 28 April 1944. This was just the beginning of many staff changes during May and June 1944.[12]

With a view to making further community contacts, the Red Cross workers asked the Catholic church in nearby Chipping Campden and the Protestant church in Blockley to select about thirty-nine mothers whose sons were serving overseas. These were to be guests of the patients at a Mother's Day party. This turned out to be a very successful event in May with many local mothers arriving in an army truck with armloads of flowers. Also some thirty-five children from a local school arrived and entertained the patients with some splendid folk dancing.

As the hospital settled down there were limited changes during April to June. The pathways between the wards and other buildings had overhead covers constructed.

The excellent cooperation of enlisted men working on this project in the evenings, combined with help received from the area engineer, contributed greatly to the ultimate success in the rapid completion of the task which was heretofore impeded by lack of available personnel.

Top secret orders were received on 27 April, by those that needed to know that D-Day was imminent. All units involved were to be ready to move from 10 May 1944. Many personnel were transferred in preparation and hospital units practised mass arrivals and evacuations.[14]

As May drew to an end and D-Day approached, 327 Station Hospital took on a new function and with it a great deal of personnel changes. Firstly the CO Colonel Roberts

Accommodation area of Northwick Park 327 Station Hospital, showing the brick buildings and Nissen huts.[13]

A US Army Military
Police guard at a
camp checkpoint.[17]

was replaced by Colonel Benny Alfred Moxness. Older and more experienced medical officers were replaced by younger and less experienced MOs. General service men trained as technicians and specialists were transferred, to be replaced by previous combat personnel who were now designated as being for limited assignment.

Perhaps the biggest change was that 327 Station Hospital had its status changed on Thursday, 1 June 1944 (five days prior to D-Day) to an American Red Cross Unit Hospital to work under the control of the International Committee of the Red Cross (ICRC). The hospital was to be both a rehabilitation hospital for American casualties and a prisoner-of-war hospital. It was re-designated in the official records as Hospital 232, though the Americans continued to use its US registration number of 327.[15]

No awards or citations were made to the hospital personnel at this time, but 402 Purple Hearts were awarded as well as five Oak Leaf Clusters to American casualties who were patients in Northwick Park during the past three months.[16]

Several changes occurred under the new commanding officer, Colonel Moxness. The Red Cross staff were asked to move into the nurses' quarters, as was the hospital dietician. Miss Verna Emanuel, who had only recently arrived on 28 April 1944, asked to be transferred to the 168th Station Hospital to be associated with her former Assistant Field Director, Mrs Augusta Noyce. On the very eve of D-Day, 5 June 1944, Miss Gwendolyn Fuller arrived to replace Miss Verna Emanuel as recreation worker.

The Red Cross report for June states that 'We managed to buy eight hundred doughnuts, which we served with coffee to the hospital personnel on D-Day.'

The patient numbers rapidly increased as patients were transferred from other hospitals to make way for the many casualties from the French beaches. Miss Fuller, recreation worker, wrote: 'Let the trainloads of patients roll in, we're ready for them.'

Miss Verna Emanuel reported:

I arrived on the 5th, on the 6th (June) everyone began working overtime … so we kept the Red Cross building open from 9pm to midnight serving doughnuts and coffee to the hard-working detachment men, officers and nurses whenever they could drop in for a few minutes.

The rehabilitation program continued and patients were encouraged to become ambulant as quickly as possible. Outside entertainment was used as well as movies three times a week.

As trainloads of wounded soldiers arrived at the American hospital in Cirencester, there were also German and other Axis wounded prisoners. These POWs were rapidly filling Northwick Park 327 Station Hospital.

The Red Cross report continued:

> The hospital has a large number of German Prisoners of War. The Assistant Field Director discussed this situation with the Commanding Officer, regarding our services to them. It was his decision that we should give them cigarettes until they get PX rations, but no comfort articles. He also OK'd giving them old magazines, chess and other checker games. Other than that, we have nothing to do with the POWs.

On Wednesday, 20 September the hospital was re-designated to be for POWs only. The Red Cross personnel felt then that they would be withdrawn from the outfit, but the commanding officer hoped that possibly at least two of them would stay as the hospital was the only US hospital within a radius of 30 miles. Colonel Moxness was of the opinion that the Red Cross were needed to service the few American patients left and the detachment men who would remain. Orders were received to evacuate all American rehabilitation patients so that the vacant beds could be utilized for the prisoner-of-war patients.[18]

Miss Gwendolyn Fuller's report of September recalls these events. She wrote:

> It was Wednesday afternoon, September 20th at the 327 Station Hospital. The Red Cross was packed with walking patients – very few had to remain in bed. The craft shop was humming and this week for the first time in nine months, the … sounds in the dayroom were shut out of the office by a fine new wall that had just been completed. With an eye to Christmas gifts, a woolly dog project was gaining momentum.
>
> Tuesday, Thursday and Saturday movies were scheduled. Friday was to be another bimonthly dance that all were looking forward to with enthusiasm. Then on Wednesday afternoon a rumour was whispered on the QT that all walking patients were to be discharged the following morning, Thursday 21st.
>
> We were to lose all our favourite patients in one fell swoop, so very suddenly. Sick at heart we watched them return to their wards to pack. The hospital was to be turned over, completely instead of partially, as it had been, to German prisoners.
>
> On the Saturday following, 23rd September 1944, the hospital was placed under the jurisdiction of the 15th Hospital Center.
>
> It remained only to see our last American patients off, which we did in fine style. They were to leave by truck Thursday morning, beginning at 7.30. The sight of all four Red Cross workers at breakfast at 7.00 was rather a jolt to the mess hall.

We planned to give each man a carton of cigarettes as he left. But this was only the beginning, since we happened to have breakfast with the PX officer and tell him of our plan he opened his storeroom and gave us candy bars and life savers and cookies and matches for all, asking us to distribute them. As they climbed into their trucks, we filled our arms with stuff and handed it out as we bade them farewell.[19]

Despite many letters from the CO to the head of the American Red Cross for some of the Red Cross personnel to stay, all four Red Cross women were transferred to Northern Ireland to join a new hospital.

The hospital remained at Northwick Park under the command of Col B.A. Moxness until the third week of June 1945. Whilst the Americans administered the camp, which the records at this time indicate was the first, if only, POW hospital solely for Germans and their Axis partners, the hospital used a largely German medical team to look after the casualties. The reader is reminded that Camp 185, Bourton-on-the-Hill, had a great many German medical staff including doctors, nurses and stretcher bearers. As the POWs' health recovered they were transferred out to other camps in Gloucestershire.

The remaining American medical and administration personnel were now transferred to a new 3,000-bed convalescent centre in Toul in France, again named Station Hospital 327 and attached to 820th Hospital Centre. Col Moxness (at this time still the CO at Northwick Park) sent a letter on 18 April to Miss Moss, American Red Cross, Paris, France, requesting at least six Red Cross workers and he names and requests the ones who had served at Northwick Park. This request was denied. The new hospital was ready to function from the end of March 1945 with intent to offer American patients maximum care for a thirty-day convalescence.[20]

The American personnel were replaced by British medical and administrative personnel and the POW hospital at Northwick Park was now officially Camp 232 under the control of the new CO, Lt Col William John Robertson P/14375 of the Royal Army Medical Corps. Lt Col Robertson was promoted to a full colonel on 15 December 1945.

Colonel Robertson was born on 18 February 1892 and served in both the First World War and the Second World War. He saw service in France, India and West Africa with the Royal Army Medical Corps before taking up his post at Northwick Park on 21 April 1946 until April 1947. He continued in administration in Northern Ireland until his retirement on 28 April 1955. He died on 13 October 1964 at Musselburgh in Scotland.

Recent research on the German personnel who died and were buried in Gloucestershire during the Second World War sheds further light on the history of Northwick Park. The list of German casualties numbers 161, with approximately thirty-one identified as dying at Northwick Park. Many of the deaths are said to have occurred 'In Hospital'; other entries give the deaths at Blockley or ambiguous place names, all of which could well have been Camp 232.[21]

Most of the German POWs and others who died in the county (totalling about eighty-six) were originally buried at Cheltenham Cemetery until an agreement was made between the UK and the Federal Republic of Germany to move the graves of German servicemen and civilian internees of both wars to a new military cemetery at Cannock Chase, Staffordshire. The Volksbund Deutsche Kriegsgräberfürsorge (German War Graves Commission) arranged this work and the cemetery, holding over 5,000 German and Austrian servicemen and women, was opened on 10 June 1967.

Looking at the deaths recorded at Northwick Park, some sixteen can be positively confirmed as occurring at this hospital during the period 20 June 1945 to 1 December 1947. The deaths of two German POWs at Northwick Park POW Hospital 232 were reported in the *Cheltenham Chronicle* of 14 June 1947:

> OTTO TITAL, Unteroffizier, died at Blockley after a Bull attack on 23rd May. Death by misadventure was the verdict returned by the North Gloucestershire Coroner, Mr J.D. Lane.
>
> Tital, who was working for a Devonshire farmer, Mr G. Reed of Longmead Farm, Bickington, Newton Abbot, in October 1946, was detailed to water the bull which was secured in a shed … Dr. Horst Pane, a German POW, said that although Tital regained some use of his limbs, he remained completely helpless and his internal injuries did not improve.[22]

Otto Tital was brought up to Northwick Park from South Devon for further hospital treatment. This would indicate that Northwick Park Hospital was still an important centre for urgent German hospital treatment and still fully functional in 1947.

Recorded on 20 September 1947:

> German POW OTTO WIEDEMANN, Stormmann, died from accidental drowning on 17th August 1947. The Coroner, Mr J.D. Lane, said 'That some supervision should be provided when German POWs bathed in a lake at Northwick Park, Blockley … whose body was dragged from the lake on August 18th after a bathing accident the night before. The Coroner observed that as long as bathing was permitted in the lake at all hours, he thought there should be life-saving appliances and some supervision.[23]

With fewer and fewer German patients to treat and an active German repatriation scheme, Northwick Park camp was eventually handed over by the War Department, between 1947 and 1948, to the Ministry of Works and the Ministry of Health. A Ministry of Health report dated 1946–52 entitled 'Proposal for New Hospital and Medical School at Northwick Park' shows that consideration was being given to maintaining and improving medical services at Camp 232.[24]

With a pressing need to provide resettlement camps for Polish displaced persons, the camp was handed over to the Polish Resettlement Corps in 1948. This Polish camp was finally closed in 1968 and today the site is a business park.[25]

12

Camp 263

Leckhampton Court, Cheltenham

Leckhampton Court Camp 263 SO 945 193, 12 June 1950.[1]

1939–1945: EARLY HISTORY

Leckhampton Court was requisitioned by the War Office in 1939 and relinquished in 1948. The property was unoccupied in 1939 and in need of repair. The building and grounds were first occupied by the Durham Light Infantry from 9 August 1940 following their retreat from Dunkirk.

The officers were garrisoned in the manor house and other ranks in the new Nissen huts.

The United States Army took over occupation of Leckhampton Court on 16 July 1942. Most of the Americans were office staff of the Signal Corps, part of the Headquarters Services of Supply for the European Theatre of Operations (ETOUSA). They worked offsite at Benhall Farm and only returned in the evenings for their meals and their accommodation in the Nissen huts. Mickey Rooney, the Hollywood film star, was billeted at Leckhampton Court for a short period prior to his transfer to London. The Americans stayed at the camp until D-Day, 6 June 1944.[2]

The officer commanding the United States Army in Cheltenham and those at Leckhampton Court was Lieutenant General John Clifford Hodges Lee (1887–1958). He was known by his colleagues as 'Jesus Christ Himself' after his initials and in reference to his devout Christian beliefs. Lt Gen. Lee was second in command after the supreme commander, General Eisenhower.

The camp at Leckhampton Court remained unoccupied after D-Day and for the next fifteen months until 7 September 1945 when it became a German POW camp, No. 263. It was then filled to capacity with 450 POWs housed in thirty-nine Nissen huts. The camp guards were from the British Pioneer Corps.

This group of Axis prisoners comprised 432 Germans, four Austrians, one Hungarian, one Dane, seven Belgians, one Rumanian and four Poles; of these, 162 were under-officers and protected personnel (PP). They were divided into: 240 army, ninety-seven air force, forty-six navy, sixty-three SS, one RAD and three civilians.[3] The German Spokesperson was named as Fw. Emil Scharfenberg 92593 and his assistant was S/Fw. Karl Batz B21690.

In addition to the POWs within the main camp there were also 199 German prisoners in a nearby hostel (not identified in the report) who had their own administration, camp leader and spokesperson.

The commandant of Camp 263 was Major A. Harris who had been the CO at Sudeley Camp 37 (there on 20 July 1945). What records exist for Major A. Harris would indicate that he was originally in the Territorial Army and transferred to the Pioneer Corps from the Gloucestershire Regiment on 3 August 1943.[4]

All of the above prisoners were captured before D-Day and they had come from Camp 8, Mile House Oswestry, Camp 177 Warth Mills at Bury, and Camp 200 in Abergavenny, Wales. Both Camp 8 and Camp 177 were reception and transit camps indicating that these prisoners had arrived from overseas.

Fortunately there are two very good accounts of the camp and its facilities. The first report is that of the International Committee of the Red Cross (ICRC) who inspected the camp on 15 September 1945 just a week after it opened. The ICRC inspector was Mr Bieri whose job was to inspect the camp in relation to the Geneva Convention. The second description is given by the Leckhampton Local History Society (LLHS).

The ICRC inspector reported:

This camp [is] situated in a beautiful area comprising of 39 Nissen huts:

19 huts are accommodation (24 men per hut)

5 huts contain wash basins and toilets

1 hut is the kitchen

2 huts are refectories/canteens

2 huts are the infirmary (one of those is empty)

1 office

1 workshop

1 canteen and hairdressers

4 accommodations, not used

2 are in a bad condition, not used.

These [huts] are heated by electricity and stoves.[5]

The report from the LLHS concludes …

> The great majority of the POWs were accommodated in Nissen huts in the grounds, to the left of the driveway going up from the Lower Lodge. The camp kitchen stood in front of the entrance gates of the Court and below it was the motor transport pool. The huts to the right of the driveway housed … a tailors and carpenter's workshop, a theatre, the medical centre, the chapel, washrooms and toilets and the administration and camp leader's hut.[6]

At this early stage there were no German medical or dental personnel; any care needed was carried out by British military medical officers. The infirmary had one Nissen hut, which was used as a sick room with twelve beds, and it also had a dispensary. The second hut was being repaired and was linked by a covered passageway. A German medical corporal, San.Uffz. Franz Istinger 602778, was responsible for the infirmary and being one of the protected personnel he was allowed to wander freely outside the camp perimeter.

Whilst there was a football pitch just outside the camp the POWs were not yet provided with a football and requested the ICRC inspector to help in providing one. No instruments for the camp orchestra, no books in the library yet, no film shows and no education were available at the time of inspection.

The ICRC report ends with these conclusions:

This camp will become one of the better ones in the region. We have met prisoners who are satisfied to be here. They have said how much they are satisfied with their relative liberty, their agricultural work where they aren't guarded or overlooked and that they will do everything possible to justify the confidence that the Commandant of the camp is showing in them. Given that these prisoners work outside the camp since 10th September 1945, it's surprising to see how much they have been able to undertake in improving their camp; the weeds which were invading have been pulled up, the huts have been cleaned and repaired etc.[7]

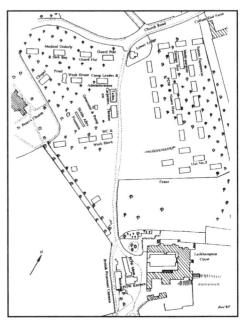

From map of Gloucestershire dated 1954 with additional information supplied by LLHS.[8]

1946: FURTHER DEVELOPMENTS

The camp continued in its development over the next four months and now housed 415 prisoners in the main camp and a further 200 in two hostels. The Germans built a pond, fountain and garden near to the church, St Peter's. As an inspection report of 20 February 1946 records, 'This is indeed one of the better camps of the country and is located in a splendid area. Morale is excellent and everyone is merry and of good mood.'

The camp leader's assistant was now O/Fw. Ernst Krieter B39686. The majority of the prisoners were working an eight-hour day in local farms or on road repairs or forestry work. For this work they were paid at a rate of 1½p an hour. As it was a punishable offence for any POW to have British currency in his possession they were paid with plastic tokens with which they could purchase items from the camp canteen. The POWs were also given fifteen cigarettes a week which was the official ration but could also purchase more from the canteen. Some entertainment was now available with a radio installed and film shows every fortnight.

O/Gefr Erwin Engler B2818 was a POW from 8 October 1944 until his release in England on 18 May 1948. He was one of five German soldiers to marry whilst in Camp 263. Erwin's sister, Traute, was a civilian working for the German Navy in Gotenhafen (Gdynia in Poland) and later transferred to near Kiel. Erwin wrote several letters to his sister, which have survived; they are now in the hands of his son,

Peter, who has kindly agreed for them to be reproduced here. Several extracts have been included to demonstrate the life and anxieties of the common German POW.

Peter provided this information about his father:

Erwin Engler was an ethnic German from Schöneck (Skarszewy) in the Polish Corridor south of Danzig (Gdansk). The area had been ceded by Germany to Poland after the First World War in 1919. He was born in 1922, technically a Polish citizen, but became a German after the occupation of Poland in 1939. He was conscripted into the Reichs Arbeitsdienst (a paramilitary work service organisation) [RAD] as soon as he completed his apprenticeship in February 1941, just prior to his 19th birthday. He spent nearly a year building Luftwaffe barracks and runways in the east before being conscripted into the German Army in December 1941. He saw action twice on the Russian front, including the winter of 1943/44, with both tours of duty ending when he sustained wounds.

Following his recovery for the second time, he was sent to the western front in France in September 1944. He was captured by General Patton's troops in eastern France on 8th October 1944. After capture the Americans removed everything of value from him including his watch. He recounted many times the image of an American sergeant who had watches up both of his arms. As the American camps were full, he was handed over to the British and on 1st November 1944 was sent to Southampton. He was held in Devizes, Belfast and Liverpool before being sent to Leckhampton. The exact date is unknown but the earliest mail still in existence from Leckhampton is dated March 1946.

The following letter from Erwin to his sister is dated 7 April 1946 and demonstrates the worry concerning no news from his family and the frustration he felt at being a prisoner. He writes this letter from his billet on a farm at Northleach:

My dear little sister,

After a year and a half of fearing for all your lives, I am happy to at last be certain that you are still alive. Tell me, Traute, were you evacuated at that time from Gotenhafen? How are things there, are you healthy and are you working? Do you by chance know what has happened to our dear mother and the others and where they are now? It would be the greatest joy for me to now find that out. My letters that I have written back home have so far all remained unanswered. I was captured on 8 October 1944 and was brought to England. I am working here on a farm. Healthwise I am very good, which I also hope for you. A comrade of mine has already been released. Please write to him … When I am released I shall come to you. Let us hope that it won't last too much longer. Now all the best until I next hear from you. With best wishes, I remain your Brother Erwin.[9]

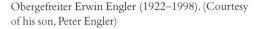

Obergefreiter Erwin Engler (1922–1998). (Courtesy   Postcard letter from Leckhampton
of his son, Peter Engler)   Court, Camp 263.

On 24 June 1946, Leckhampton Camp took over the administration of Camp 142 at
Brockworth and its hostels. This included Quedgeley Court with its 116 prisoners,
Shurdington with forty-two, Woodchester with forty, and Brockworth itself with
sixty-eight men. In addition to these hostels, another at Northleach was opened with
fifty German POWs newly arrived from the US.

The commandant, Major A. Harris, was very aware that these newly arrived prisoners had not yet been assessed as to their political beliefs; he therefore requested
the COGA re-education inspector to conduct a prisoner screening. Mr A.T. Duff
of the COGA was in Gloucester at this time, evaluating the new German POWs
arriving at Staverton and Quedgeley RAF POW camps. The inspector duly arrived
and attended on 10/12 and 15/17 July 1946.

In reference to Hostel 142 Brockworth Mr Duff reported that:

> The general complexion of POWs taken over from camp 142 is grey/black.
> They had been held in captivity in the USA and most had undergone a certain
> amount of re-education with the result that the present opinions of about 33% of
> them (those in the B- category) are the result of this re-education and seem rather
> superficial; they are just converted from black but a long way to go yet. 26% are still
> black, although they have been subject to the same re-education; their beliefs have
> been slightly shaken on some points but in the main they have retained their faith
> in National Socialism, its aims and methods. The two C+ prisoners believe Hitler to
> have been right in every respect and would fight for his cause again if they got the
> chance. POWs in the B category, 33%, are mainly non-political, labourer-type and
> of low intelligence. The B+ POWs, 6%, totally reject National Socialism but have
> not yet found anything positive to put in its place. The 2% whites are idealists who
> have always condemned Hitler on moral grounds; they were very passive whilst
> with 142 as they seemed under the impression that their views got no support but
> they are quite prepared to play an active part in camp life. The one prisoner graded
> A- is a definite anti-Nazi but he is a querulous type, full of criticism of the Allies.[10]

The German hostel leader at Brockworth was H/Fw. Hugo Schumacher, aged 34 and a professional soldier since 1934. He was described as quite non-political and holding no real opinions on anything, not much personality, Grade B.

Regarding Northleach Hostel, Mr Duff reported:

> The political complexion of the intake to this hostel is very black. The POWs have been held in many different camps in the USA and do not seem to have been touched by any re-education at all. 20% are C+; completely faithful to Hitler, convinced that Germany's cause in the war a just one and claiming that all means are justified which contribute to the attainment of Germany's 'natural rights'. 50% are grade C; they still believe National Socialism to be good although they are just a little doubtful as to the moral rightness of some of Hitler's actions. The few B grades are men who either reject National Socialism for its failure or else are quite non-political. None of the POWs in the intake has any really positive or morally sound outlook on life.[11]

The German hostel leader at Northleach was O/Gefr Walther Amtsberg, aged 24, a clerk by profession. The report describes him as efficient, intelligent, opportunist, with very little political understanding. An easy tool in the hands of the 'Blacks' (graded as C/C+ and still Nazis) in the hostel and should be changed as soon as a more suitable man can be found. Grade B+.

Mr Duff of the COGA also reported on his visit on 28/29 July 1946 to Hunt Court Hostel, just off the Shurdington Road. There were 180 prisoners at Hunt Court, having arrived on 19 July 1946. Most had been captured in the final weeks of the war and all had been held by the Americans but in UK camps. Mr Duff's report grades these men as being mostly 'Grey'; most were older men, 102 being over the age of 35. He states:

> Almost all of these older men were classed as being non-thinking, labour types, of low intelligence and quite apolitical, being prepared to follow any lead which will give them work. Most graded B. The few graded as Black are to be found amongst the younger men; they are still Black because they have been brought up on National Socialism and know nothing else. In contrast to the B's, they are intelligent and seem very eager to learn and understand more about politics. The two Whites are anti-socialist of very long standing, one an ex-Communist youth leader who has turned Socialist, and the other a man who has spent 31 months in a concentration camp for his anti-Nazi activities.[12]

These POWs at Hunt Court had not received any re-education in the past eighteen months of American captivity. They were left entirely to their own devices during any free time they had and now showed no initiative to be re-educated. They showed little interest in anything except the prospect of repatriation.

The Hunt Court hostel leader was O/Gefr Werner Hausweiller, a 28-year-old metal turner by profession. A pleasant personality, quiet demeanour and anti-militarist; he was camp leader at Shrivenham under the Americans. Shows little interest in re-education as it has never come within the scope of his activities. Graded as B+. [13]

Another letter from Erwin Engler to his sister is dated 28 April 1946. He has now received news that his family is alive and together:

> … On Easter Monday I received a letter from Schöneck in which Erich informed me that they [Erwin's family] were all together and still alive. A return address was not given, but I will write back nevertheless.

2 June 1946:

> … I am healthy and am also satisfied with the food. Nevertheless I long to be released and leave barbed wire behind me forever. In fact I do not know where I will then settle. As my occupation will especially be in demand however, I am not too pessimistic.

Erwin was a qualified building cabinetmaker in Germany and the nearest English equivalent would be a joiner/cabinetmaker. On 28 July 1946:

> … We who have lost everything should realise that our future will not be a bed of roses. Then as long as we don't also lose the courage to face life, we will pull through, of that I am convinced. I still want to explain so much more that I would need 10 such letters. I have already written to Dad and Hilli [Erwin's cousin]; none of the people from Schöneck have contacted me up until now.

On 19/20 October 1946, the camp was visited by the English inspector who had travelled from London and stayed at the Ware's Hotel in Cheltenham. He was visiting to monitor and guide the Germans who were studying English at beginner, intermediate and advanced levels. There were a total of twenty-three students on this occasion at both the main camp and Brockworth Hostel. [14]

The next COGA report shows that the camp commandant, Major A. Harris, had left and been replaced by Lt Col. F.S.S. Lamprey. The British interpreter was Staff Sergeant Horton. The camp strength in October had risen to 1,456 POWs:

Main Camp	335	
Shurdington	45	1 hut
Quedgeley Court	102	House and huts
Brockworth	115	Nissen huts
Elmbridge	267	Concrete houses & huts

Elkstone	60	Huts
Chesterton	52	Nissen & concrete huts
Northleach	58	1 hut
Woodchester	38	1 house
Siddington	246	House & Nissen huts
Hunt Court	19	Nissen huts
Billeted on farms	119	

The German camp leader in October 1946 was H/Fw. Franz Albrecht 562001, graded B+. He was 36 years old, a civic surveyor by profession. Mr Duff records him as a simple soul: 'His political knowledge is very limited and he plays no active part in re-education.' The deputy camp leader was O/Fw. Karl Wolf B191666. He was 33 years old and an ex-policeman who had been transferred to the German Army. Described as 'A straightforward type but with small understanding of politics'.[15]

Further information on Karl Wolf is given by the Leckhampton Local History Society who wrote:

Sgt. Karl Wolf served in an Infantry Regiment as an engineer, mainly in construction. He saw action on several fronts, including Russia, but was captured in the last few days of April 1945 … Karl came to Leckhampton Court with practically nothing apart from his clothes; everything else had been 'liberated' from him by his American captors.[16]

The movement of prisoners was to be the pattern from now on as more and more Germans were repatriated home. The result was that German teachers, musicians, actors etc. were moved, resulting in many activities being curtailed.

Erwin Engler was still billeted at Northleach when he heard news that his 'girl-friend Hilda' was to be engaged to another. 'This certainly upset me but now I am over it. After all I am not the only person this has happened to.'

On 22 September 1946:

… I have resolved to brood about it [Hilda] as little as possible, yet it is not possible to dismiss all such thoughts out of one's head. Whether I shall succeed I do not know. They want to start with the repatriation of the prisoners of war and in fact they should have finished in two years' time. Now I hope I shall not be one of the last.

On 17 November 1946, Erwin received yet more bad news when he was informed that his family was being split up and sent to work in various locations in Poland. On 2 December 1946:

… Who would have thought that I would actually have to spend three Christmases in captivity? The likes of us have not intended to think about this day; however this intention is in vain. Spontaneously thoughts pass into the mind, as one thinks back in terms of one's childhood and of the hours spent under the Christmas tree, unspoilt and with a heart full of bliss. Locked away from one's loved ones at home, on such days, one lives only on memories. One feels lonely, yet I believe only those who don't have such memories can be sad. We hope therefore to dwell in our thoughts with our loved ones over Christmas and hope that they enjoy the best of health. Above all we hope for a reunion. With best wishes to you and Günter, I remain your brother Erwin.

⚡— 1947: RESTRICTIONS ON POWS EASED —⚡

In early January 1947, Erwin Engler was transferred back to the main camp at Leckhampton Court.

The restrictions on the prisoners were gradually being reduced as Erwin recalls:

We have received permission to go further from the camp. Yesterday I made use of it for the first time and must say it was a genuine relief for me. Although it is only January, we are having the most beautiful spring weather.

On 28 January 1947, several questions were raised in the House of Commons relating to the repatriation of German POWs.[17]

Mr Skeffington-Lodge asked the Secretary of State for War, Mr Bellenger:

Whether he is yet in a position to announce either a speeding-up in the direct repatriation of prisoners of war in North Africa, or a scheme for bringing them to this country with the object of including them in the release arrangements already made for their fellow countrymen.

Mr Bellenger replied:

I hope that from the beginning of July the rate of repatriation will be accelerated to 5,000 a month. Any scheme for moving prisoners to this country for inclusion in the repatriation arrangements here would only result in delaying their repatriation instead of accelerating it.

Mr Sorensen then asked the Secretary of State for War how many prisoners of war were now in this country; how many have been repatriated; how many have been transferred from Canada and elsewhere and whether any were still to come; how many of these are between 14 and 18 years of age; what is the incidence of sickness;

and, in view of the effect of protracted imprisonment on morale, whether the present rate of repatriation will be substantially speeded-up in the near future.

Mr Bellenger responded:

There were 355,224 prisoners of war in this country at the end of December. 60,668 have been repatriated since the scheme began on 26th September last year. Since that date 4,221 have been transferred from Canada and none from elsewhere. There are no more to come. Regarding the age of prisoners of war I would refer my hon. friend to my reply to him on 29th October 1946. The incidence of sickness is one per cent, or under. In the immediate future repatriation will continue in accordance with the programme laid down by His Majesty's Government.

Mr M. Lindsay then asked the Secretary of State for War what steps were being taken to induce German prisoners of war in Britain to defer their repatriation. He replied:

As the hon. Member was informed by my right hon. friend the Minister of Labour on 19th November, German prisoners of war are normally given the opportunity, when their turn for repatriation comes, to defer their repatriation for six months, but no inducements are offered them to defer.

Mr Byers then asked the Secretary of State for War the rate per month at which it had been possible to repatriate German prisoners of war from this country, up to the last convenient date.

Mr Bellenger informed Mr Byers that repatriation under the present scheme started on 26 September 1946. The following numbers had so far been repatriated:

26–30 September	2,418
October	14,803
November	15,429
December	14,236
1–25 January 1947	13,782
Total =	60,668

The monthly average was 15,167.

The camp was visited by Mr Duff of the COGA on 22/23 January 1947: his objectives were to present a re-education report to the War Office as well as to undertake further screening at two of the hostels. There were now 1,477 POWs with 342 at the main camp, and two of the hostels – Northleach and Shurdington – had now been closed.

The camp interpreter, Staff Sergeant Horton, was reported as fully co-operative in all matters concerning re-education of the German prisoners. He was said to take an active interest and gave his full support to the POWs who ran the re-education activities. Mr Duff put in his report that S/Sgt Horton was overburdened with administration duties and his involvement in the re-education programme was 'relatively' small.

Helmut Oppel, grade A, was the German re-education leader for the main camp and the hostels. Aged 23, he had been a surveyor in civilian life before being conscripted into the SS. He had attended two courses at the training centre and Mr Duff recorded that he was:

> … very keen indeed and gives his whole time to re-education. Rather young but understands what is wanted and has developed his political knowledge and a gift of speech and puts both to good use. Editor of the camp newspaper and Leader of the Political Discussion group.

Helmut Oppel had considerable help from Karl Rueger, grade B+, aged 45. Karl had been a businessman in civilian life and Mr Duff reported that he had supported re-education all along and this despite his poor political record and his strong trait of nationalism. Karl held the position of the camp librarian and also co-editor of the camp newspaper.

Helmut Oppel had been allowed by the camp CO, Lt Col F.S.S. Lamprey, to devote his full time to the work, although already a member of the camp police. The underlying principle of the re-education programme had been the correction of the Nazi perversion of German history and the German characteristic of blaming others for his political shortcomings. The methods used to achieve these objectives were the formation of a political discussion group in the main camp and most of the hostels (as had been found so successful at Camps 61 and 37), and the holding of regular press reviews.

Oppel himself visited each hostel in turn at intervals, giving lectures in each and finding fellow POWs to keep the re-education activities going. The British staff played a relatively minor role in the re-education programme but they did give their fullest support to Helmut Oppel and his colleagues.

Mr Duff, the COGA re-education inspector, was concerned about the state of the POWs' morale in January 1947. He wrote:

> Morale has fluctuated very considerably of late, being very easily affected by temporary circumstances. There is a feeling that repatriation is going too slowly in this camp, the direct result of the repatriation of a large number of Whites from the nearby Camp 37 [Sudeley] about which POWs are well informed. Further, the town of Cheltenham had been put out-of-bounds by the CO because of the presence of a large number of Polish soldiers' camps in and around Cheltenham; POWs had not been informed of the reason for this restriction and felt that they were being unfairly treated. This is being put right by an explanation to all POWs. A third factor upsetting morale is what POWs consider to be unjust restrictions on the use of fuel and the consequent shortage of hot water …[18]

Life in the camp continued to improve as further restrictions on the prisoners were eased. The LLHS wrote:

> In April 1947 a recital of organ and church music was given by POWs to a packed St Peter's church, and in the summer a small group was taken to observe Cheltenham Town Council in session. Further visits were made to other places – the Museum and Art Gallery, Toc 'H', the Salvation Army, the Society of Friends and the Cheltenham Trades Council. A party of volunteers refurbished the Parish Hall, distempering and painting it over several weeks … in June 1947 the Rector thanked the prisoners for their magnificent efforts and the camp band provided music during the refreshments and dancing that followed.[19]

Erwin's letter of 13 April 1947:

> I have recently received the surprising news from Hilli [his cousin] that she will shortly be released to go back to Germany. I am delighted for the girl she has sat there long enough, only in doing this I dare not think of my fate.
>
> Freedom is one's most valuable possession, whatever happens. I have still not received any news from our Mum although already it is a long time since I wrote to her. I cannot explain it.
>
> I am enjoying the best of health and am working again though for a market gardener. I like it better there than on the farm, however I would much rather be working in my trade.

Erwin was working for a Mr Rudge, who became a lifelong friend to him. The market garden was close to Cheltenham Racecourse, where he was to meet his future wife.

Erwin's letter of 27 April 1947 is the first one that was no longer restricted:

> As I have become aware that they have at last allowed us to write a normal letter once a month, I will take the opportunity of sending one to you. Having said that, I have not got the slightest idea of what to write to you … Yet this is all trivia, if only I had a sign of life from our Mum. From one day to the next I long for a sign and when I come home from work in the evenings, I am always forced to realise with regret again, that no letter is lying on my bed. Always when I think again of Mum and little Friedel [his 12-year-old brother], I am of no use to anybody. Despite that, I am still not giving up hope of hearing something from them yet. Otherwise I am well, that is to say what a person behind barbed wire can call well. The weather here is exceptional now, inviting one to go for a walk. Unfortunately in the town there are many Polish soldiers and when I see them, the whole Sunday afternoon is ruined.
>
> For today I shall close.

The camp was visited on 27 May 1947 by the ICRC representative Mr E.A. Aeberhard. The camp, together with its hostels and billetes, now numbered 1,643 POWs with two medical officers. This is a short report that includes the usual comments on camp facilities and the state of the POWs' medical health, according to the Geneva Convention. It does, however, report the death by suicide of Friedrich Stuenkel, a 41-year-old soldier, on 18 December 1946. He was buried in the military section in the cemetery at Cheltenham.

Included with this ICRC report are details of visits to Brockworth, Hunt Court and Elmbridge hostels.[20]

Brockworth Hostel
1 In charge: NCO Staff Sergeant Box.
2 Camp Leader: H/Fw. Hugo Schumacher B196604.
3 Hostel Strength: 184 POWs including 2 patients and 2 in the detention block.
4 Description: 24 Nissen huts including 13 dormitories. 22 men per hut. All amenities.
5 Clothing: Insufficient supply of working clothes.
6 Labour: Ministry of Works and Agriculture.
7 Camp Infirmary: Capacity 20 beds. Medical staff: Dr. Anselm Lessman 523480, with 1 dentist and 2 orderlies.
8 General Impression: Nice Camp and very good Camp Leader.
9 The hostel had one of its huts converted into a bakery and now supplied bread to Leckhampton POWs.

Hunt Court
1 Camp Leader: Uffz. Joseph Guettle B193712.
2 Camp Capacity: 150 men. To-day's strength: 47 men.
3 This camp had an average strength of 100 POWs and will now be disbanded in a few days.
4 The Camp Leader was satisfied with treatment, food, clothing and dormitories (single beds).
5 General Impression: It was a good hostel.

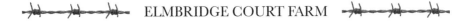 ELMBRIDGE COURT FARM

Elmbridge Court Farm was initially used by the War Department as a searchlight battery, possibly in connection with Staverton RAF base to its north. With the influx of so many German POWs after the hostilities in Europe, a very large camp was built at Elmbridge housing up to 350 German prisoners. The camp was built very close to the farmhouse in an adjacent paddock, with the camp extending to the Gloucester–Cheltenham railway line.

Elmbridge Court, 12 April 1947.[21]

(The farm was once surrounded by a moat and access to this historic farm and the POW camp was via Nine Elms Road. Sadly the farm and its surrounding buildings were later demolished in order to build the Barnwood Link Road (A40/A417) just south of a new Golden Valley by-pass and roundabout sometime in the 1950s. A new farm named after the demolished building was built to the north of the original towards the Elmbridge Court Government Offices.)

As with Leckhampton Court it appears that the German prisoners very quickly made Elmbridge Camp 'shipshape', growing both vegetables for the kitchen and flowers to improve the camp appearance. It was very well managed with dinner every day at 7 p.m. At first the 'Gestapo', who were also imprisoned there, caused all kinds of problems. They would not mix with the 'ordinary' soldiers and refused to work with them.[22]

Rosemary Cooke, who was born at the farm and lived there as a child, remembers the camp and was able to give an account of some of the events that took place there.[23] She recalls that the photograph [on page 156] was taken from her bedroom window and says:

The view from Rosemary Cooke's upstairs window, Elmbridge Court. (Courtesy of Rosemary Cooke)

> Since the photo was taken from the upstairs window in the front of Elmbridge Court you can see how close the camp was to our front door. The double hedge conceals the moat which continues left in a circle around the house ending in double driveways on the right where it was filled in long ago. This entrance to the house was used by vehicles as there was a narrower path just to the right of the hedge which we used all the time. The entrance was just to the right of the long building with three windows and all traffic had to go along our lane between the house and farm buildings …
>
> I believe there had been fences or wire around the POW camp but it was very low security as the prisoners were quite happy to sit out the war and as far as we know, no one wanted to or did escape. There was a parade ground in front of the elms and a recreational hut with a stage.

Of the picture Rosemary comments that:

> The camp [was] now in its last stages, having been used as a 'Displaced Persons' camp and then by the Land Army before lying empty for several years. The camp was demolished just after this picture was taken.

Elmbridge POW Hostel was for 'other ranks' and the prisoners were expected to work under the terms of the Geneva Convention. Most were happy to do so but not in all cases. It was the responsibility of the War Agriculture Executive Committee (WAEC) to allocate the prisoners to work on local farms. Seven POWs were sent to Zoon's Court Farm, just a short distance away on the slopes of Churchdown Hill. One prisoner refused to work with the other six, creating disharmony within the group. As in other cases of non-compliance, such prisoners were quickly segregated from their comrades and transferred to more secure surroundings at another camp.

Rosemary reported that when the Germans were told of their repatriation they were also informed that the camp would be used by displaced persons. This did not go down well with the Germans, who then basically wrecked the camp. They proceeded to:

… dig up all the gardens they had planted and tended during their internment because they hated the Bolsheviks – Russians, Ukrainians and Lithuanians – and had no intention of leaving them a well-organised, functional camp in pleasant surroundings that they had created.

It would appear that some of the Germans had a pet hare and when vacating the camp released this tame animal. Rosemary told the author that her brother approached this hare only to find that it did not run away and was most affectionate. It then became a family pet on Elmbridge Court Farm.

The ICRC report gives the following summary:

1 In charge: Staff Sergeant Mellon.
2 Campleader: Fw. Walter Lehmann 590399.
3 Hostel Strength: 345 POWs including 3 PP, all German.
4 Description: Altogether 9 Nissen huts and 5 barracks, 24 men in each Nissen hut, double bedsteads, two blankets and one sleeping bag. Twice weekly showerbath, all amenities.
5 Food: Sufficient.
6 Clothing: Now better.
7 Convention: A German copy was given to Camp Leader.
8 Labour: Principally farm work.
9 Canteen: Enough supplies.
10 Complaints: No complaints.
11 General Impression: Good Hostel.[24]

Erwin's next letter is dated 8 June 1947 – after hearing that his sister wants him to send her what were prohibited goods:

I have just this minute received your dear letter and thank you with all my heart for it. It was the first mail that I have received on a Sunday. I am very sorry, my dear little sister, yet what causes me most pain is that I am unable to help you. Only rationed groceries can be sent to Germany from here and we POWs cannot get them. Non-rationed ones cannot get through. You see, Traute, we are certainly allowed out, however we are not allowed to set foot inside shops. Anyone who has got any English money finishes up in the guardhouse. Also no food is allowed to be brought into the barracks, it is all very strict. When I think of you and the others, I could cry. That I must disappoint you so is more difficult for me than anything else has ever been.

On 7 July 1947:

… Our POW income is very meagre; we earn 5½ shillings a week. For that we can buy 20 cigarettes and a piece of cake. One must hang on to the remaining pennies in order to be able to buy toothpaste, shoe polish etc. In any case I will try to send you a small package in August. Hopefully I shall remain healthy until then. Dear Traute, there is nothing about of my 'imminent' release, it will take at least a year. I have written to the Polish Red Cross about Dad and also about Mum. I hope that I get a reply from them. Unfortunately I cannot do any more from here.

On 9 July 1947, German POWs were given permission by the British Government to marry. One diary entry, written by a former POW at Leckhampton named Gerd Heida, records that on 10 July Heinz Eckert became the first German to marry his long-term girlfriend. The bridegroom nevertheless still had to return to camp by 10 p.m. on the day of his wedding. Leckhampton POW Camp 263 was to see five POWs marrying local girls and remaining in England after the war.[25]

On 6 September Erwin wrote:

… I don't know whether I should dare hope that my package is already there when this letter arrives. In fact many of the same are being sent back because thread is in them. In fact no one has said before that it is forbidden to post these, hence the surprise. So we will hope for the best, won't we dear sister?

Erwin had hatched a plan to help his sister. He had been working unofficially in his spare time in a local drapery to refurbish the shop. The draper offered Erwin money, but instead Erwin asked to be paid in reels of cotton, which he intended to post to his sister as they were valuable on the German black market. At that time there were restrictions on what German POWs could send to Germany, but reels of cotton were not on the list. Several weeks later cotton thread was officially blacklisted, however, Traute did receive the reels and they helped her and her husband to survive hard times.

The letter continues:

Healthwise I am very well, which I hope also of you. Releases have increased recently, at the moment it is Group 19's turn. I belong to Group 22 and reckon on about six months until my release. Hopefully it will not be too cold in the forthcoming winter, and then travelling really is no fun in freezing weather. In this connection I still have a gutful from Russia.

Now I have another little surprise for you. In fact I have got to know a young lass here. She is a very nice girl and my only regret that she is English. At this time that does not play any role. In any case she helps me get over the lonely hours of captivity. Last Sunday I borrowed a bicycle and cycled with her into the country.

She had brought a hearty food parcel with her, which was probably the most important thing. In any case it was the most wonderful day of my captivity.

Although still anticipating repatriation, Erwin announced that he had met a woman named Ursula, who later became his wife.

Mr Duff of the COGA paid a re-education inspection visit to the camp on 23–26 September 1947.

The repatriation process was speeding up as many of the general public, together with many clergy and other prominent citizens, were becoming vocally opposed to the continuing custody of German POWs. The total strength of the camp was now down to 830 men, with 347 having been recently repatriated. The report also records that one German POW was at this time in Gloucester Prison.[26]

Main Camp	251
Brockworth	71
Quedgeley	51
Woodchester	25
Siddington	199
Northleach (reopened)	64
Billetees	168
Gloucester Jail	1

(The Shurdington, Chesterton, Elkstone, Elmbridge and Hunt Court Hostels were closed.)

Lt Col F.S.S. Lamprey retained his position as the CO and the interpreter was still Staff Sergeant K.C. Horton.

With many German staff being repatriated there were some changes in the camp personnel. The camp leader was now O/Fw. Karl WOLF, grade B. Mr Duff describes him as a non-political, quiet and decent man, who has made a good job as leader. He does everything possible to further re-education. The deputy camp leader was Soldat Willi Mueller, grade B.

Mr Duff reports that his reception was good with full co-operation forthcoming in all respects. The CO 'is not really interested in re-education at all and dislikes all Germans, but he places no obstacles in the way'. Whilst the report is favourable to the effort made by some German POWs towards the re-education of their comrades, Mr Duff makes his concerns known about the state of the POWs' morale:

Morale is fair to good throughout the whole camp. Headquarters and some of the hostels are in a very satisfactory position as regards making civilian contacts and POWs take full advantage of all privileges. The occasionally rather stern and anti-German attitude of the CO, some minor friction with NCOs in some hostels, and poor news from home in the mail, are the only things adversely affecting morale at the moment, and these not very seriously.

Of the POWs, 20 per cent were under 25 years of age and presented no problems to the camp and its organisation. They participated in all the camp activities and had contact with youth organisations in both Gloucester and Cheltenham. Thirty of these younger prisoners were away at a Youth Camp at the time of Mr Duff's inspection.

Many of the POWs now had some expectation of their eventual repatriation and volunteered for extra work on many of the local farms in order to acquire additional finances prior to returning to Germany.

The re-education activities continued at the main camp and hostels though numbers were affected by those working in the evenings. Lectures were provided and, whilst most were warmly received, one visiting German lecturer received a hostile reception to his talk on 'Denazification'. The lecture did more harm than good apparently as the POWs felt that it was an attack on them. 'The lecturer himself did not go down well either as he tended to harp on the fact that he had the good fortune to be "English" now.'

The POWs made several outside contacts and visits up to September 1947, including:

Regular visits to the Salvation Army
Regular visits to Toc 'H'
Regular visits to the Society of Friends
Meeting of Cheltenham Trades Council
Meetings of the Cheltenham Town Council
Three visits to the Cheltenham Museum and Art Gallery
POWs from Quedgeley hostel attended a meeting of the Gloucester Town Council
Regular visits to the Gloucester City Youth Centre
Regular visits to the Youth Club in Cheltenham
POWs from Siddington paid three visits to Cirencester Council
Visit to Gloucester Cathedral.

Erwin Engler's next letter is dated 19 October 1947:

… I am pleased that you have received the 'package' and that it has made you happy. Now if I hadn't taken on work off my own bat, I would not have come to think of such a thing, of course. Now it is impossible, unfortunately, because it gets dark too early. From your letter I take it that none of the contents were missing.

Next I would like to be excused for my long silence. The letter and the card caught me by surprise – in the guardhouse in fact! They landed me with three weeks this time, it was a bit much but now it is over. You should not think badly of me, dear sister, it was actually only a trifle. Having said that, when one has lived a life bound by rules and regulations for nearly seven years, something like that means nothing and now most importantly, a big surprise, Uncle Carl wrote to me that he had got a letter from our Mum. She is back together with Friedel after they had been separated.

The POWs were allowed two hours of recreation each day during which they were allowed to go into Cheltenham or to do any additional work to earn extra money. However, the POWs managed to leave and re-enter the camp virtually whenever they wanted, but it was a matter of a disciplinary charge if they were caught. There was a barbed wire fence surrounding the camp but this was basically just a perimeter fence and offered very little difficulty to the prisoners should they want to leave.

Erwin's letter of 23 November 1947:

… Now to your questions. Actually it is my business how often and for how long I have been inside the guardhouse, don't you think? You should know so that you are reassured, so up until now, only twice.

Tell me Traute, what do you mean by leave? POWs do not get leave. Certainly when one goes through the pickets at night, and gets caught doing it, then one has had leave granted as it were, mind you, not to Germany. You understand don't you?

They have published a new repatriation plan now, whereby my release group's turn will be in the middle of May. At the same time they have given us the opportunity of staying here as civilian workers. A few from our camp, mainly homeless, have already made use of this.

Otherwise, under the circumstances, I am well. I am as fit as a fiddle, which is certainly the main thing.

This is an interesting letter from Erwin to his sister. Her questions to him would imply very little understanding of the restrictions placed on a prisoner of war. He refers to the chance of staying on in England as a civilian worker. Labour was in such demand after the war that Germans living in the British sector of Germany were being recruited as potential labour within Britain.

Siddington Hostel with its 199 men and Woodchester with twenty-five POWs were taken over by Camp 124 at Wapley, near Yate in South Gloucestershire, in November 1947, and Coleford Camp 61 was made a satellite camp under the administration of Leckhampton. Leckhampton also took over the two hostels of Coleford Camp 61: Churcham and Highnam.

On 10 December 1947 Erwin wrote:

Now I have something pleasant to tell you. You may perhaps have heard that the Minister for War has permitted us POWs to have two days' Christmas leave. My Ursula has got in touch with her father and he has invited me. You will hardly be able to imagine how pleased I am, after over three years, to be able to have unrestricted movement at last. By the way, he lives in the town where Shakespeare lived; it will certainly be a great joy for me. Hopefully – after all that is the critical point – I will get permission from the Commandant. Otherwise I am well under the circumstances.

The acting commandant did give Erwin his approval for Christmas leave.

Mr A.T. Duff visited Leckhampton Camp on 5–17 December 1947 for a re-education survey on behalf of the COGA.

The camp strength was now three officers (all medical staff) and 1,332 other ranks:[27]

Main Camp Leckhampton	313
Coleford Camp 61 sat.camp	486
Quedgeley Court	36
Brockworth	80
Northleach	60
Churcham	33
Highnam	160
Billetees	167

The Main Camp personnel remained as previously reported with the exception of Staff Sgt K.C. Horton, the camp interpreter, who had been demobilised just prior to the visit. Mr Duff recorded that: 'This is a considerable handicap as he was the only person who really put himself out to help re-education.' He continues:

> The CO's attitude towards POWs is strictly military and he shows no real understanding of the problem of re-education. The attitude of the CO at the satellite camp is poor and has caused a drop in morale there.

The repatriation programme had speeded up by December and as a consequence camp morale was reported as being very good. Some concern, however, was felt by those POWs whose homes were under Russian occupation. As Erwin had written, POWs could now send parcels home and the fact that they could do this made them feel that they could help their loved ones.

The morale at Coleford had deteriorated after being taken over by Leckhampton. Apparently Mr Duff concluded that this was due to a much more strict discipline imposed by Lt Col Lamprey. The POWs at Coleford felt that the previous CO had a much better understanding of their needs.

The POWs at the main camp at Leckhampton showed considerable interest in what was going on politically, both internationally and in Germany. By this time they had free access to the radio, including broadcasts from Hamburg, Berlin, Leipzig, Frankfurt and Munich in Germany, as well as national and some European newspapers.

Mr Duff made the following observations:

> The general attitude of the POWs is one of 'wait and see' and the whole political situation is regarded as being governed by the tension between east and west. POWs do not trust Russia and dislike her methods; politically they lean towards a socialism

based on the ideas of the west but they have very little confidence in the ability or desire of the western allies really to help Germany, and they show a tendency to see underhand motives in British policy now; this is the almost direct result of the putting into force of the dismantling plan. The reason given by the British for carrying out this plan (except insofar as armament factories are concerned) is not generally accepted and the elimination of commercial competition is seen in many instances; this is reinforced by reports received in letters from home. Press reports of a reply by the British Foreign Secretary to the MP (Mr Stokes) in the Commons recently disclaiming any sympathy with the Germans is taken as a further indication of the real British attitude. There is an almost general rejection of the party politics now going on in Germany. The 'Congress of the German People' is seen as a Russian puppet show and is not regarded as representative.[28]

Training courses for selected German POWs were still being run at Wilton Park, Beaconsfield. Five prisoners had already attended, with another two ready for the next session, and a further eleven Germans recommended for future courses. With only a few sceptics these courses were looked upon favourably, with regular volunteers ready to undertake them.

The re-education activities were ongoing but were suffering from the constant movement of POWs through the camp either as transfers or to be repatriated. During December, 300 POWs were transferred up to Scotland.

Apart from the visits outlined above, discussion groups and invited speakers, it was decided to run a camp parliament, as this had been very successful in the Coleford Camp and hostels. The first elections were to take place in the immediate future.

Letter from Erwin Engler, New Year's Eve 1947:

… The day before yesterday I received a letter from Erich with the news that upset me deeply. I don't want to believe it and yet it is true that our beloved mother fell asleep forever on 17th August 1947. May God grant her the eternal peace that she certainly earned? Her final companion, whom she had with her during the most difficult time of her trouble-filled life and who no doubt has been her only comfort – our little Friedel [aged 14] – is now wandering around all alone somewhere in this world. [Erwin's mother died in Potulice, a Polish concentration camp.]

According to Erich's assumption, he should be in the Russian Occupation Zone. It is our duty to adopt him. Therefore I ask you dear sister to do your utmost to locate him as quickly as possible. I shall also try to do so, but I believe you will have quicker success. In fact I have heard that Ivan [Russian] abducts orphan boys of Friedel's age, whether it is true, I don't know, in any case it is necessary to do this quickly. I have been busy thinking recently of staying here as a civilian worker, perhaps for a year. I would then get the normal wage of an English worker; I could get a few clothes during this time and would be able to help you with parcels etc.

I believe quite a few things would result especially as my girlfriend Ursula has a circle of acquaintances of really kind people. Look dear sister, put aside the yearning for a reunion and think about this logically. What could I do for you or Friedel anyway, if I were to come back to Germany possibly in April? I would then have nothing to wear apart from my POW clothes. I would certainly find work but with that one does not get far and I am an orphan with black marketeering. As I said Traute, I am of the opinion that I could do a lot more for you from here.

Now to something else to give you the full picture. Perhaps you will not be able to understand, in any case I am not joking. Ursula is in fact my wife to be. She is the sweetest girl whom you can think of and she has also been the one who six months ago has made me human again. She has not been ashamed to go out with me with my POW patches; on the contrary she has comforted me when people have pointed their fingers at us. In any case I am proud of her and she is of me.

She has your nature, in fact she reminds me of you in many ways. As I have already told you, she asked her father to invite me for Christmas. As he is an architect and she is his only daughter, you will certainly be able to imagine that with my still broken English, I had a bloody hard nut to crack. By the way, he is a very nice person and I shall never forget the two days I spent at his house.

So little sister, now I have explained everything to you by opening my heart to you. You must not think, by God, that I am there just for my Ursula and want to stay here on these grounds. She will go to the end of the Earth with me, even to Germany. You know me and know that I have a hard school of life behind me and that I consider every risky step carefully before I move on. You have always understood me and will understand me now, won't you? Please tell me your thoughts but consider them thoroughly.

In the hope that you will have found Friedel soon, I will close.

Erwin's son Peter remembers his father telling him that 'when going out with Ursula, it often happened that someone would spit at Ursula saying, "You bitch, you should be ashamed talking to a bloody Gerry," and sometimes even worse things.'

 1948: THE FINAL MONTHS

On 5 February 1948 the camp strength stood at 1,724 POWs. There were 362 in the main camp, 1,134 in hostels and 228 in billets.

In Erwin's letter dated 15 February 1948, he tells his sister that his English girlfriend is now pregnant but he has been denied the right to stay in England. Erwin always believed that it was the commandant who had refused his request to stay in England and there is some evidence that this belief was justified. Fortunately for Erwin, the government extended its policy allowing trained German personnel to stay in Britain.

(The British Government actively sought skilled Germans within the British sector of Germany to work in Britain.) Erwin Engler had a definite offer of work, was skilled and had the backing of his girlfriend's family, which was to be his eventual salvation.

As certain events have recently occurred affecting me, which I really had not considered, I shall now tell you something that I actually wanted to explain later. Briefly I am in a pickle and right now do not know how I shall get out of it.

As I have already told you, at first I wanted to marry as a civilian. For certain reasons however I must do it now, in fact as soon as I get the approval to do so. It would not have been difficult; however our Commandant has not approved my staying here. It's true I won't give up hope yet, perhaps something can be done from the other side, it is doubtful though. In the event I have to return to Germany now, I mean for release, I shall try to return to England again. In the event this will not be possible for me, I shall let Ursula come to Germany. True the last is difficult, firstly due to the meagre rations and secondly I must have a house to get it approved.

Ursula cannot count on possible help during the time of her inability to work; in fact Mr Father-in-law has become very disappointed. On those grounds I am very sorry, but now nothing can be done to change things. So now you know, dear sister, how things are with me. I understand that I have done something that in many respects I should not have done, it is unfair to Ursula and the child on the way. There is however no point in reproaching myself, I will not do that either. I am determined to do my best, only it is so sad that they put so many obstacles in our way. Perhaps those concerned would understand things somewhat better if they had also lived behind barbed wire. Perhaps it was also not quite right on the one hand to give us a certain amount of freedom and on the other hand to ruin our plans. This is not meant to be an excuse however, although it sounds like one. There will certainly be a way forward, don't you think so too?

Now I want to close. I hope that I have described everything to you in enough detail and also have not concealed anything. Perhaps you are also disappointed with your 'older and stupid' brother, I don't know.

Erwin and Ursula did not require the commandant's permission to marry and so were married at the Cheltenham Registry Office. He wrote to his sister on 13 March 1948:

… You will understand when I tell you that on 9th March Ursula became my little wife. Of course there was a heap of things to take care of. I was only free for the wedding during the day, and had to be back in the camp by 10pm as usual. Now we have it all behind us and are both happy.

I have never in my life seen a happier person than Ursula was on our wedding day. If she will always hold on to me so as she has done so far, then I cannot wish for anything better for me. I am very sorry that you can't get to know her; she is so quite different from the other English girls. I would like to describe her better to you but I am no poet or writer. She understands me like nobody has understood before, when she looks me in the eyes, she knows what I want. We are well suited to each other.

The one wish I have is to be able to stay here. It has not been decided up until now, however I hope it will …

Ursula's father worked very hard to obtain Erwin's release, with letters sent to the relevant government departments, the commandant at Leckhampton Camp and also trying to secure him employment. He told the commandant in one letter that 'I might be able to arrange work in Warwickshire or Buckinghamshire if a transfer could be arranged'. He also requested that Erwin be granted leave in order to attend interviews etc.

It would appear that these requests fell on deaf ears as the CO, Lt Col F.S.S. Lamprey, had Erwin transferred to a hostel in Tortworth near Falfield in the south of the county.

Mr Duff of the COGA paid his final visit to Leckhampton Camp on 1–3 and 9 March 1948. He compares the positive and negative feelings of the POWs between those being repatriated to the American and French zones in Germany and those going to the Russian zone.

The strength of the camp and its remaining hostels is given as 1,337 men, being three officers and 1,334 other ranks.[29]

Main Camp Leckhampton	319
Springhill satellite	491
Quedgeley Court	43
Brockworth	84
Churcham	25
Highnam	234
Billetees	141

Of the above numbers of German POWs, two were listed as 'A' grade protected personnel and all other prisoners were now graded as 'B'. The number of those having been repatriated through Leckhampton Court since the December report is given as 505 POWs.

Personnel:

CO	Lt Col F.S.S. Lamprey
Interpreter	Capt. H. Grenville and Staff Sgt Sacki
Camp Leader	O/Fw. Karl Wolf
Deputy C/L	Sold. Willi Mueller
German MO	U/Arzt Max Waag

Hostel Leaders:

Brockworth	H/Fw. Hugo Schumacher
Quedgeley	O/Sch.M. Martin Stichel
Highnam	O/Gefr Werner Hausweiller
Churcham	O/Fw. Peter Becker
Springhill	Fw. Helmut Roehl

Mr Duff is very critical of the CO. His report states that:

> The CO has no interest in re-education but puts no obstacles in the way of the work. His own attitude towards Germans is one of dislike and in his dealings with POWs he is strictly military and unnecessarily harsh at times.

The report is a survey of the German attitudes and proceeds with those within the main camp who were selected at random and were to be repatriated to the Russian zone:

> Generally speaking, the attitude of the majority of POWs is one of indifference towards the British, although there is a small percentage of POWs whose attitude is friendly; of the latter, however, in most instances the attitude is based on purely materialistic considerations and [they] regard the British only in a friendly light in proportion as to what they can get out of them for themselves. There is a very small number of thinking POWs whose friendly attitude is non-materialistic and results from enlightenment through re-education. For the great majority Germany is always the first thought and the emotional tie is so strong that reason is ousted; very little thought is given to anything except their own and Germany's advantage.
>
> There is no evidence whatsoever of hate or any desire to do deliberate harm to the British; there is little evidence of outright dislike, but there is considerable distrust resulting from the treatment they have received as POWs. There is a very strong tendency on the part of POWs to see only the mistakes that England has made and to forget or ignore anything positive. They do, however, go so far as to admit openly that they believe in England's good intentions towards Germany and volunteered the information that they think that the treatment of Germany would probably have been much worse if France or Russia had had the sole say.
>
> POWs claim that there is very little in the way of life which they would like to have in Germany. The majority of them have done agricultural work during the past three years, voice very sceptical opinions about British agriculture, which they regard as definitely backward. From this they deduce ill-will on the part of the British; if good intentions were really there the British would recognise agricultural production and bring it to a high state of efficiency to meet the world food shortage and thus help Germany …

The German POWs gave their reasons for distrusting the Allies and the reasons for their indifference:

1 The British profess ideals of humanity which they have not carried out towards POWs. Under this heading POWs have listed: The treatment of POWs in the camps in Belgium; the fact that POWs ex-USA, who had been promised by high-ranking US officers that they were going home to Germany, were brought to and kept in England; the treatment these POWs received on arrival in England – the taking away from POWs of personal property purchased in the camp canteens in USA. [The proportion of the POWs supporting these views was high.]
2 Screening. The attitude of individual screeners and the type of questions asked are still strongly criticised by the prisoners. They can see no connection between the questions and the resulting grade. Further, many maintain that the majority of those graded as 'A' and sent home first were bad types; the wrong men were released first. [Again the proportion agreeing with this was high.]
3 Want in Germany and bad news from home. POWs cannot understand why the western allies allow such a situation to drag on and why they do not do more to help. POWs are convinced that resources are available but that goodwill to utilise them is lacking. [Proportion high.]
4 The bad influence of a section of the British press is very noticeable. POWs show a strong tendency to pick on and remember those news items and articles which feed their feelings of self-pity. They like to regard themselves as 'Slave Labour'. [Proportion high amongst average POWs, but small amongst the thinkers.]
5 The attitude of the USA towards Germany is regarded as being solely determined by selfish economic (big business) considerations. [Proportion high.]

The POWs were then asked to assess the reasons why they appreciated and liked the British. The remarks that follow were given by those almost exclusively labelled as thinkers by Mr Duff. He admits that the proportion of such men was now very small in the camp due to the repatriation programme.

1 Racially and intellectually Germany is closer to England.
2 British public opinion has been on the side of the POWs; many prisoners see in the pressure of public opinion stimulated by their own complaints to the public the sole reason for the speed-up in repatriation.
3 Enlightenment by all the means re-education has had at its disposal.
4 Friendliness of the local civilian population (Cheltenham).
5 The fact that POWs may send parcels home to relieve the extreme need of their families.

Mr Duff records his general conclusions drawing on his extensive involvement in re-education in the prisoner-of-war camps of Gloucestershire:

These conclusions with respect to this camp (Main Camp 263) are generalisations from observations over a considerable period of time (since May 1946) by this training advisor. Observation of a fairly constant group has only been possible in the case of those POWs actively engaged in the running of re-education in the camp, for the rest, one has been dealing with an ever flowing mass of POWs. The group running re-education has been far above the average in intellect and political interest and has, from time to time, attracted to it from the mass and directly influenced considerable numbers of thinking POWs, but its influence on the mass has been indirect as far as it has been successful at all.

The results of re-education have been good in the case of the small proportion (hardly ever more than 20%) of thinking POWs (usually of higher intellect and education). The results have not been so marked with the bulk of prisoners, whose outlook is influenced for the most part by purely materialistic considerations; they still judge exclusively from the standpoint of what they, as individuals, want, and they seem unable or unwilling to adjust their desires for the good of the whole. They are essentially selfish and lacking in ethic. The success or not of re-education has depended much on the receptive capacity of the individual and his ability to see himself and Germany in the proper relationship to the cause and hard fact of Germany's present position. The mass feels frustrated and tends to see the cause of this frustration in ill-will, or at least lack of good-will, on the part of those who conquered Germany. The average POW accepts no responsibility for himself or for Germany (except that Germany lost the war) for the present situation of his country and tends to see it as imposed on Germany from without rather than having come from within. The responsibility of the individual for the way in which his country or government acts is a thing the average POW finds very hard to grasp or believe – he has not yet got over the feeling that might automatically confers right. It has been very difficult to overcome this way of thinking, and going ahead with good example is probably the only way of really influencing it. The lack of the spectacular in democracy leads the average POW to think that it is not working. Re-education has a lot of work to do still and much patience will be needed.

Mr Duff returned one week later, on 9 March 1948, to conclude his report. The objective he gives is 'to obtain reactions of a further group of POWs who were in repatriation transit'. POWs were assembling at Brockworth hostel from all the other hostels and from Springhill satellite camp as they waited to be repatriated to the American and French zones. There were approximately 100 at the hostel.

In sharp contrast to the POWs in transit to the Russian zone seen in the Main Camp, these prisoners exhibited a much more positive attitude towards England. They are definitely of the opinion that their enforced stay has been beneficial to the individual, whether he knows it or not, and they bear no ill-feelings towards England and the English despite the mistakes which they claim have been made in the treatment of prisoners and in policy towards Germany. They realise that all peoples make mistakes; whatever errors England may have made, they are not to be held against her, as they feel that the intentions of all (with the sole exception of some of the military personnel with whom they have come into contact) have been good and genuine.

As far as politics are concerned, there is a strong tendency amongst them to want to withdraw and leave the field to those who 'understand politics' – they have not rid themselves of the feeling that politics are something mysterious beyond the under-standing of the average individual and they tend very much to think that the individual cannot possibly have any influence on high policy. The English parliamentary system is admired, but POWs do not think such a thing possible in Germany owing to the multiplicity and mutual intolerance of the German political parties, and express the wish that political life as it is in England could become possible at home.

It must be remembered that a very substantial percentage of these lower-ranking Germans being questioned were in their 20s with little knowledge of the world except that taught to them by the Nazis under National Socialism.

The POWs interviewed by Mr Duff gave a number of reasons why they held negative views towards the English military personnel and their treatment of them. With the exception of Leckhampton Court Camp 263, the comments that were recorded about the camp commandants were on the positive side with most COs described as being fair and compassionate. The CO at Leckhampton, Lt Col F.S.S. Lamprey, however, was not regarded in a good light either by the German POWs or by Mr Duff of the COGA. An almost unanimous response to a question on their dislikes was recorded as: 'Dislikes: Only in connection with the treatment they have received at the hands of military personnel, in particular the attitude of the CO of Camp 263 towards them.'

Most of the POWs were prepared to give the English the benefit of the doubt. By and large they admitted that the re-education programme had been successful, particularly amongst the POWs who did not come from the Main Camp 263, where the personal attitude of the CO seems to have had a disproportionately adverse effect. They reported that they thought the English temperament was better and they appre-ciated the meaning of tolerance shown by the English, 'despite his [the Englishman's] apparent laziness in particular to agriculture'. They recorded that the English attitude towards life was better for the individual and all of them felt that in general they agreed that they all had learnt a lot during their stay in England.

Another comment focused on the friendliness of the local Gloucestershire people and many of those present stated that they wanted to keep up their connections with their friends in England. There are many accounts of reciprocal visits after the war by ex-POWs and those they befriended whilst in England.

In his final conclusions Mr Duff devotes a paragraph to the CO, Lt Col F.S.S. Lamprey. He writes:

His personal attitude towards the Germans is one of dislike and towards POWs he is strictly military. He is a professional soldier on the point of retirement. He is of a rather nervous and unstable disposition and has a tendency to see deliberate crime in the smallest misdemeanour; this makes him at times unnecessarily harsh in his disciplinary action and unduly insistent on a military attitude. POWs know he dislikes them and make allowances for it; what they dislike is the seemingly unnecessary military attitude.

Lt.Col. Lamprey is not personally interested in re-education but he has never placed any obstacle in the way of its activities and has cooperated with the training adviser on all occasions. The civilian population of the town of Cheltenham (in which the camp is situated) is rather sentimentally disposed towards POWs and consequently antagonistic towards the CO. This reacts both ways.[30]

The next letter from Erwin Engler was from the Tortworth Hostel near Falfield, Gloucestershire, on 11 April 1948:

I was very pleased to receive your letter with Friedel's address [Erwin's little brother]. I still cannot believe that the little fellow is there. Let us hope that he can come to you soon. I still have not heard from Erich for a long time. As he has moved, he will have a new address, would you please give it to me?

There is not much to say about my wedding. We saw the registrar at 11.30am, had an appointment with a photographer, and then we went into the country. At 8pm we returned and went to her Aunt's [Ursula's aunt lived in Prestbury] where we demolished the wedding cake. The cake came from Ursula's step-mother. At 10pm I had to be back in the camp again. On another day I was given a German style cake baked by the camp baker, which was admired by many people. I was especially proud because I was the first POW to receive a cake from the kitchen.

Unfortunately they have dealt me another blow just before the midnight hour in that they have transferred me here. Now it won't be long, at any rate, before I am free. I can still hardly imagine how it is when one is freed moreover from something one hates so much.

Erwin was then transferred to Camp 124/a Ashton Gate near Bedminster, Bristol. This had been a large German working camp but was now being used to house those awaiting imminent repatriation to Germany. Within hours he would be leaving England, and with it his new wife.

Bedminster, 2 May 1948:

Actually the weather today is so good, it is a pity to sit in the hut and write letters, but when one has too much time, one loses the will to go for a walk.

I have been in Bristol for a week, right in the city. In the meantime I have looked around a little, but in all honesty since I have been sent away from Cheltenham, I have lost the will to do anything. We are not working anymore, and so the days seem even longer. Only two transports are left behind, which in eight to fourteen days will leave from here, everything else has gone. I should have gone with the first one. In fact in Cheltenham they ruined my plans, yet, at the last moment a new order was issued, under which my wishes were to be taken into account. After this order I was then working at my trade in the camp. I hope that the final decision is here within the next week. It has cost a lot of effort; it has been the reward of not only me but also of everyone, my father-in-law and a few of his relatives or friends. As they are all educated people like lawyers, rectors and teachers, I have sometimes sweated when writing letters, yet until now I have always succeeded. So let us hope that I shall have achieved it soon, I mean to become a civilian, and then I can also think of you more often. I am really sorry that at the moment I cannot help you, in fact I am not earning any wages, but as soon as it is possible for me, I shall do what I can for you.

Hopefully you will have Friedel at your house soon; it will be a great relief for me to know this. Now dear little sister something else. Please don't write to me at this address any more. As I do not yet know where I shall be going, I shall propose that you send my letters to Ursula, she will forward them to me …

Another change of national policy came to Erwin's aid. German POWs who had married British women and had a trade could, if they so wished, stay in Britain. The CO at Bedminster camp was aware of Erwin's predicament and appears to have been sympathetic to his plight. He completed the required forms supporting Erwin's request to stay in England. Erwin was transferred back to Leckhampton with recommendations for his early release.

Erwin's father-in-law had not been idle, as the following two extracts from his correspondence show:

14th May 1948 to The Under Secretary,
Aliens Department, Home Office.
I understand that your department deals with the applications for civilian status from German prisoners who, having married English girls, desire to stay and work in England … My anxiety is heightened because the man has now been retransferred to Leckhampton Court, Camp 263, Cheltenham. I do not wish to say more in this letter than that I am not alone in feeling grave dissatisfaction with the official attitude, military and civil, in Gloucestershire to German POWs which is in marked contrast to that in other camps and districts. When previously at Leckhampton, he missed, through official non co-operation, earlier civilianisation, and a good job and billet which I had at much trouble secured for him. Meanwhile, he will not be earning or, alternatively, may be sent to some other job from which it may be difficult to extricate him.

I understand that his political record is all right. If there is anything else against him, I consider that, as his father-in-law and possibly responsible for the maintenance of his wife, I should be told at once.

14th May 1948 to The Under Secretary of State,
The War Office.
…While I express appreciation of the attitude of the Bedminster camp 124, I am most dissatisfied with the contrasting treatment at the Cheltenham 263 camp to which I understand the man is now retransferred. Through uncooperative obstruction, whether of military or agricultural committee I do not know, this man's civilianisation has been delayed and a job promised him 6 weeks ago fell through. I have now a job and accommodation waiting for him and have been standing by all week to take him there. I do not intend this job also to fall through. As we have written military assurance that the man will eventually be civilianised, I presume that his application must have been accepted. But I give you to understand that any attempt to repatriate this man in spite of it, will immediately be raised at Cabinet level and I have friends who will not hesitate to do so. If I do not get confirmation of Engler's release tomorrow, Saturday, morning, I shall immediately take further steps at higher level.

Erwin Engler B2818 was released on Tuesday, 18 May 1948 at 10.58 a.m. He was informed by Captain Grenville, the camp interpreter, that his release was fixed for 11 a.m. and that if he was not off the premises by that time he would be locked up for disobedience. Whilst this may well have been said with 'tongue in cheek' Erwin told his son, Peter, that he ran the 200m to the camp gates. Apparently there was nobody available to repay Erwin the money that he was entitled to and so he left captivity as a German POW penniless.

It was nine days later on Thursday, 27 May 1948 that Camp 263 at Leckhampton Court finally closed and the last of the POWs started their journey home.

THE END OF AN ERA

By mid-1948 all the POWs in Gloucestershire had been repatriated or had been given permission to remain as civilian workers. The camps had been closed down and most sites were transferred back to their original owners or to other authorities for various purposes, some of which have been mentioned. In 2013 many of the sites cannot be identified due to urban development, forestation or total removal. At some locations there are still remnants of the buildings to be seen, such as at Northwick Park Industrial Estate. Springhill near Bourton-on-the-Hill and Churcham both have a number of huts still standing but permission from the farmer should be sought before visiting. As for Leckhampton Court, it is now a Sue Ryder Hospice; the camp huts are all gone although a few concrete hut bases can still be seen.

Notes

Chapter 1

1. www.wikipedia.org
2. International Committee of the Red Cross (ICRC) – www.icrc.org/ihl.nsf/Full/
3. Sophie Jackson, *Churchill's Unexpected Guests: Prisoners of War in Britain in World War II* (The History Press, 2010).
4. Bob Moore & Kent Fedorowich, *The British Empire and its Italian Prisoners of War 1940–1947* (Palgrave Publishers, 2002).
5. Ibid.
6. Ibid.
7. Ibid.
8. Sophie Jackson, as Ref.3.
9. Ibid.

Chapter 2

1. RAF/106G/UK/1480 frame 4067, 9 May 1946. English Heritage (RAF photography).
2. ACICR report, C SC GB / Sudeley camp number 37, 23 July 1942.
3. Some memories of the war years 1939–45 by Mr L. Willett, Winchcombe Local History project.
4. Bob Moore & Kent Fedorowich, *The British Empire and its Italian Prisoners of War 1940–1947* (Palgrave Publishers, 2002) p.25.
5. The Diaries of the Bishop of Clifton 1932–48 (The Catholic Archives, Clifton, Bristol).
6. ACICR report; as Ref. 2, 25 July 1945.
7. Ibid.
8. COGA report SUDELEY 152/43 FO 939/119 (The National Archives, Kew).
9. ACICR report; as Ref. 2, 21 February 1946.
10. Ibid.
11. Ibid.
12. COGA report SUDELEY FO 939/33, August 1946 (The National Archives, Kew).
13. Ibid.
14. ACICR report; as Ref. 2, 28 May 1947.
15. COGA report SUDELEY FO 939/337, April 1947 (The National Archives, Kew).
16. Coroner's report on Ewald Issel Ref. CO2/1/3233 – 3234 14/28/3.
17. US/7GR/LOC349 frame 3041, 27 May 1944. English Heritage (USAAF photography).

Chapter 3

1. RAF/CPE/UK/1913 frame 4015, 30 December 1946. English Heritage (RAF photography).
2. ACICR, C SC GB / Prisoner-of-war camp number 61, 21 July 1942. Wynolls Hill (also spelt Wynols Hill) Nr Coleford, Gloucestershire.
3. ACICR report; as Ref. 2, 8 July 1943.
4. Ibid.
5. From correspondence with the author and from Internet searches.
6. With kind permission of Radio Rivista (Italian Radio Journal), February 1995, p.87.
7. Photograph of Andre Russo with permission of his daughter, Mrs Marilyn Champion.
8. RAF/CRE/UK/ 2110 frame 4418, 28 May 1947. English Heritage (RAF photography).
9. ACICR report; as Ref.2, 16 June 1946.
10. Ibid.
11. COGA Inspection Report, Wynols Hill, Nr Coleford Camp 61, 19 November 1946,

Mr Gibson. FO 939/142 (The National Archives, Kew).

12. ACICR report; as Ref. 2, 7 July 1947.

13. RAF/CRE/UK 1961 frame 3007, 14 May 1948. English Heritage (RAF photography).

14. *Citizen* newspaper, 24 and 26 December 1946. Gloucestershire Archives.

15. RAF/CRE/UK 1961 frame 3011, 9 April 1947. English Heritage (RAF photography).

16. ACICR report; as Ref. 2, 16 October 1947.

Chapter 4

1. Correspondence with Joachim Schulze relating to his article in *Tewkesbury Historical Society Bulletin* No.21 (2012): 'A Guest of HM Government 1946–48: Memories of a German Prisoner of War at Tewkesbury'.

2. All quotations and comments by Joachim Schulze.

3. RAF/SCPE/UK/1929 frame 2064, 16 January 1947. English Heritage (RAF photography).

4. War Cabinet CAB/65/50/25 May 1945, pp.358–9 (The National Archives, Kew).

Chapter 5

1. Bob Moore and Kent Fedorowich, *The British Empire and its Italian Prisoners of War, 1940–1947* (Palgrave Publishers, 2002), pp.137-147.

2. Ibid.

3. Kent Fedorowich and Bob Moore, *Co-Belligerency and Prisoners of War: Britain and Italy, 1943–1945* (The International History Review, February 1996), p. 37, paras 2–3.

4. Ibid, p.46.

5. War Cabinet Memorandum WP (43) 395. Position of Italian Prisoners of War after Armistice, P.J. Grigg. 14 September 1943. CAB 66/40/45 (The National Archives, Kew).

6. From 'The Swindon Village History Collection', Issue 1 (1996) and Issue 3 (1998).

7. RAF/106G/UK/1347 frame 5339 1st April 1946. English Heritage (RAF photography).

8. Swindon Hall. Photograph by the author.

9. D2299/7977 Swindon Hall, correspondence ref requisition 1942–43. Gloucestershire Archives.

10. The author is grateful to Lt Col J. Starling who did the original research into the war diaries of the Pioneer Corps. Also for his help in their interpretation.

11. WO/166/16131 War Diaries (The National Archives, Kew).

12. ACICR, C SC GB / Camp number 554

Swindon Hall. Dr J. Wirth. 28 April 1944.

13. Ibid.

14. Ibid.

15. Ibid.

16. WO/166/16131 War Diaries (The National Archives, Kew).

17. OS Map of Newark House and Farm.

18. WO/166/17728-649 Coy, War Diaries (The National Archives, Kew).

19. Ibid.

20. Swindon Village Local History Project, Issue 4 (1999).

21. WO/166/14083-555 Coy, War Diaries (The National Archives, Kew).

22. Ibid.

23. ACICR, C SC GB / Camp number 555 Woodfield Farm. Dr J. Wirth. 28 April 1944.

24. RAF/106G/UK/1347 frame 7366 1 April 1946. English Heritage (RAF photography).

25. ACICR report; as Ref. 23.

26. Ibid.

27. Ibid.

28. WO/166/14083-555 Coy, War Diaries (The National Archives, Kew).

29. WO/166/17704 Report by Major Rogers, Officer Commanding 555, to the Headquarters of Number 106 Group Pioneer Corps (The National Archives, Kew).

30. FO/371/49865/ZM5619 Progress Report, Italian POWs, 1–31 October 1945 (The National Archives, Kew).

Chapter 6

1. RAF/CPE/UK/2110 frame 4264, 28 May 1947. English Heritage (RAF photography).

2. John Malin, *Magic Memories and Milestones* (Blockley Antiquarian Society, 1998), p. 41.

3. J.T. Thornton, Memories of E.T.O. POW

Enclosure No. 1, Moreton History, Vol. 9
No. 3, Autumn 2004.
4. ACICR, C SC GB / Bourton-on-the-Hill
camp number 157, 17 September 1945.
5. Sophie Jackson, *Churchill's Unexpected
Guests: Prisoners of War in Britain in World
War II* (The History Press, 2010), Chapter 7,
p.p 161–71 includes a list of escaped prisoners.
6. ACICR report; as Ref. 4.
7. Ibid.
8. Ibid.
9. Some paintings and other items made by the
German prisoners are on display at the Wellington
Aviation Museum at Moreton-in-Marsh.
10. ACICR report; as Ref. 4.

11. Ibid., 14 November 1945.
12. Ibid.
13. Ibid.
14. House of Commons Debate,
12 February 1946, vol. 419 cc. 171.
15. ACICR report; as Ref. 4, 29 May 1947.
16. Ibid., 11 November 1947.

(Sadly Mr John Malin of the Blockley
Antiquarian Society passed away shortly after
this account of Camp 157 was written. He was
very helpful and very keen to see the project
completed and offered his help, advice and
recollections.)

Chapter 7

1. RAF/CPE/UK1926 frame 2157,
16 January 1947. English Heritage
(RAF photography).
2. ACICR, C SC GB / Springhill camp
number 185, 25 October 1944.
3. ACICR report; as Ref. 2, 25 April 1945.
4. Campden and District Historical &
Archaeological Society (CADHAS).
5. Wellington Aviation Museum, Moreton-
in-Marsh, website.
6. Enquiry report by email from The National
Archives, Kew.
7. Correspondence with Zosia
Biegus, author and webmaster of
www.polishresettlementcampsintheuk.co.uk
8. Drawing by German POW, supplied
by Mr Robin Dale of Manor Farm,
Bourton-on-the-Hill; given to him by a
German visitor.
9. ACICR report; as Ref. 2, 25 April 1945.
10. Ibid.
11. ACICR report; as Ref. 2, 23 January 1946.

12. Obermaschinenmatt (Senior Machinist)
Theodor Hunkirchen's papers sent to the
author by his son.
13. ACICR report; as Ref. 2, 15 June 1946.
14. German POW letter purchased via
the Internet.
15. John Malin, email correspondence
25 April 2011.
16. ACICR report; as Ref. 2, 1 June 1947.
17. Photograph of Springhill Camp supplied by
Andy Goloskof of the Polish community
(photographer unknown).
18. ACICR report; as Ref. 2, 10 November 1947.
19. Sophie Jackson, *Churchill's Unexpected
Guests: Prisoners of War in Britain in World
War II* (The History Press, 2010), pp. 170–1
(includes names and rank of known escapers).
20. Campden and District Historical &
Archaeological Society (CADHAS)
Archives: Klaus Behr's POW
diary at Springhill Camp 185,
September 1944–January 1948.

Chapter 8

1. RAF/106G/UK/1347 frame 7131,
1 April 1946. English Heritage (RAF
photography).
2. Malcolm Barrass, RAF Historical Society.
3. COGA report; RAF 702 POW Camp
Staverton, Duff 18–20 June 1946;
FO939/250 (The National Archives, Kew).
4. Ibid.
5. Ibid.
6. Ibid.
7. Ibid., Duff 9 January 1947.
8. Ibid.
9. *A History of the RAF in World War 2*,
Quedgeley Community Trust.

10. COGA report; RAF Number 7
Maintenance Unit Quedgeley,
5–6 June 1946; FO939/250 (The National
Archives, Kew).
11. Ibid.
12. Ibid.
13. Ibid.
14. Ibid, 10 December 1946.
15. Ibid.
16. Ibid.

Chapter 9

1. RAF/82/1152 frame 99, 15 April 1955. English Heritage (RAF photography).
2. Brockworth parish newsletter, April 2011. Brockworth Parish Council.
3. Reproduced with permission of Ordnance Survey Maps.
4. ACICR, C SC GB / Leckhampton number 263, 27 May 1947.
5. Audio recording of Mr I. Hewer, who spent his holidays in Brockworth during and after the war.
6. These letters in Italian were translated by Sara Tozzato.
7. Mr Alan J. Snarey, personal communications.
8. ACICR report; as Ref. 3.
9. ACICR report; as Ref. 3, 8 March 1948.
10. D2299/3056, Quedgeley Court, Quedgeley, Sales Particulars. Date 1924, Gloucestershire Archives.
11. US/7PH/GP/LOC234 frame 5036, 15 March 1944. English Heritage
12. Quedgeley news article. Unfortunately the present editor cannot confirm date or authenticity regarding Italian POW occupation.
13. D2299/3056, Quedgeley Court, Quedgeley, Sales Particulars. Date 1924, Gloucestershire Archives.
14. Hansard; January 1947. Written Answers (Commons), Prisoners of War. Vol. 432 c174W.
15. RAF/58/2958 frame 41, 19 June 1959. English Heritage (RAF photography).
16. Willy Reuter's story and photo recorded by Patrick Barrett on BBC website: www.bbc.co.uk and reproduced with his kind permission..
17. D2299/6916, Quedgeley Court, Quedgeley, Records of conditions etc. letter. Date 1940–49. Gloucestershire Archives.

Chapter 10

1. US/7PH/GP/LOC65 frame 1043, 18 October 1943. English Heritage (USAAF photography). Gloucestershire Archives.
2. D2472/2 Northway House, Ashchurch sales details by Bruton Knowles & Co., 10 June 1911. Gloucestershire Archives.
3. Email response from Mr Brian Crago, Central Vehicle Depot (CVD) Museum Curator, Ashchurch Depot, August 2012, ref. period 1939–47.
4. Ibid.
5. US Army list of units stationed in Britain in February 1944 prior to D-Day. (See D-Day Museum, Portsmouth, at www.ddaymuseum.co.uk.)
6. John Dixon, Tewkesbury in the Second World War, Tewkesbury Historical Society Bulletin No. 3 (1994).
7. Photograph of Northway House, 1911.
8. Tewkesbury Historical Society at www.gi.freeuk.com. THS maintains a dedicated website of US personnel who served at G-25 and a history of the camp.
9. Ibid.
10. Ibid.
11. Ibid.
12. Report of death of Erich Jakubzik, Gloucestershire Echo, 20 December 1945.
13. House of Commons debate 28 January 1947, vol. 432 cc173-4W.
14. ACICR, C SC GB / Northway camp number 1009, 8 March 1947.
15. All pictures of Camp 1009 included by kind permission of the son of Sgt Major Alfred Ratio Lawson of the Royal Pioneer Corps, who received them from a departing German POW in 1947.
16. Email account of Major Sweet from Lt Col J. Starling, Royal Pioneer Corps Association.
17. Tewkesbury Register 15/07/1944, p. 11; courtesy of THS Woodard Database.
18. Tewkesbury Register 30/09/1944, p. 12; courtesy of THS Woodard Database.
19. The Cheltenham Chronicle & Gloucestershire Graphic, Saturday 31 May 1947, p. 3.

(The author is most grateful to Mr John Dixon and Mr & Mrs Alan Snarey of the Tewkesbury Historical Society for their help and support, also to Mr Brian Crago for arranging a visit to the Ashchurch Army Museum.)

Chapter 11

1. Internet searches.
2. Much help was given by John Malin with his recollections of Blockley and the US Army stationed there.
3. RAF/CPE/UK/1929 frame 1108 16 January 1947. English Heritage (RAF photography).
4. OS Map of the County of Worcestershire, published 1955.

5. 327 Station Hospital History, from Supplemental History 1 July-30 September 1944; M.A. Alex 1st Lt, MAC, Historical Officer (National Archives, Maryland, USA).

6. American Red Cross reports from 6 January 1944 to September 1944 (National Archives, Maryland, USA).

7. Ibid.

8. Ibid.

9. Ibid.

10. Ibid.

11. American Red Cross reports: as Ref. 6.

12. Ibid.

13. Picture courtesy of Rysiek Sozanski.

14. American Red Cross reports: as Ref. 6.

15. Ibid.

16. 327 Station Hospital History: as Ref. 5.

17. Picture courtesy of Rysiek Sozanski.

18. Col Moxness correspondence (National Archives, Maryland, USA).

19. Gwendolyn Fuller 31752, Recreation Worker, September 1944 Report (National Archives, Maryland, USA). 20.   Col Moxness; as Ref. 18.

21. Research notes from Matthew Smaldon, 'German War Graves in the UK, 1939–48', received July 2013.

22. *Cheltenham Chronicle*, 14 June 1947.

23. *Cheltenham Chronicle*, 20 September 1947.

24. Ministry of Health. Ref. MH 89/134 1946–52. Proposal for new hospital and medical school at Northwick Park (The National Archives, Kew).

25. Zosia Biegus: 'A History of Northwick Park Polish D.P. Camp, Gloucestershire, 1948–1969' (2nd edition, 2009).

Chapter 12

1. RAF/58/505 frame 5126, 12 June 1950. English Heritage (RAF photography).

2. *Leckhampton in the Second World War*, Leckhampton Local History Society (LLHS). Eds Eric Miller, John Randall & Amy Woolacott, Top Flight Printing.

3. ACICR, C SC GB / Prisoner-of-war camp number 263, 15 September 1945.

4. Lt Col John Starling, Royal Pioneer Corps Association.

5. ACICR report; as Ref. 3.

6. Description supplied by LLHS of an ICRC report.

7. ACICR report; as Ref. 3.

8. *Leckhampton in the Second World War*, LLHS.

9. All extracts from letters written by Erwin Engler to his sister are included by kind permission of his son Peter Engler, 2009.

10. COGA report. Segregation Report Camp 263. A.T. Duff, July 1946. FO 939/183 (The National Archives, Kew).

11. Ibid.

12. Ibid.

13. COGA report; as Ref. 10.

14. COGA, English Inspector's Report, Mr E.F. Peeler, Camp 263 Leckhampton Court 1946–47. FO 939/183 (The National Archives, Kew).

15. COGA report; as Ref. 10, October 1946.

16. *Leckhampton in the Second World War*, LLHS.

17. House of Commons debate 28 January 1947, Vol. 432 cc171-3 W.

18. COGA Re-education Report and Screening. A.T. Duff, 22–23 January 1947. FO 939/183 (The National Archives, Kew).

19. *Leckhampton in the Second World War*, LLHS.

20. ACICR report; as Ref. 3, 27 May 1947.

21. RAF/CPE/UK/1988 frame 5036, 12 April 1947. English Heritage (RAF photography)

22. *Leckhampton in the Second World War*, LLHS.

23. These notes were made in interview with Rosemary Cooke who had consulted with her family.

24. ACICR report; as Ref. 3, 27 May 1947.

25. *Leckhampton in the Second World War*, LLHS.

26. COGA Re-education Report. A.T. Duff, 23–6 September 1947. FO 939/183 (The National Archives, Kew).

27. COGA report; as Ref. 26, 5–17 December 1947.

28. Ibid.

29. COGA report; as Ref. 26, 1–3 March 1948 and 9 March 1948.

30. Ibid.